Beginning Google Blogger

HEATHER WRIGHT-PORTO

Beginning Google Blogger

ISBN-13 (pbk): 978-1-4302-3012-0

ISBN-13 (electronic): 978-1-4302-3013-7

Printed and bound in the United States of America 9 8 7 6 5 4 3 2 1

President and Publisher: Paul Manning
Lead Editor: Steve Anglin
Development Editor: Brian MacDonald
Technical Reviewer: Sonny Discini
Editorial Board: Clay Andres, Steve Anglin, Mark Beckner, Ewan Buckingham, Tony Campbell, Gary Cornell, Jonathan Gennick, Michelle Lowman, Matthew Moodie, Jeffrey Pepper, Frank Pohlmann, Ben Renow-Clarke, Dominic Shakeshaft, Matt Wade, Tom Welsh
Coordinating Editor: Laurin Becker
Copy Editor: Chris Marcheso
Compositor: Kimberly Burton
Indexer: BIM Indexing & Proofreading Services
Artist: April Milne
Cover Designer: Anna Ishchenko

Distributed to the book trade worldwide by Springer Science+Business Media, LLC., 233 Spring Street, 6th Floor, New York, NY 10013. Phone 1-800-SPRINGER, fax (201) 348-4505, e-mail orders-ny@springer-sbm.com, or visit www.springeronline.com.

For information on translations, please e-mail rights@apress.com, or visit www.apress.com.

Apress and friends of ED books may be purchased in bulk for academic, corporate, or promotional use. eBook versions and licenses are also available for most titles. For more information, reference our Special Bulk Sales–eBook Licensing web page at www.apress.com/info/bulksales.

The source code for this book is available to readers at www.apress.com. You will need to answer questions pertaining to this book in order to successfully download the code.

About the Author

■ **Heather Wright-Porto** has a Master's Degree in Computer Information Systems and has had her own computer consulting company since 1995 (Premier Computer Solutions). She has trained clients on Microsoft Office, as well as Photoshop, Illustrator, Quark and other graphic design applications, in addition to developing databases (using Microsoft Access, Microsoft SQL Server, and Oracle), programming in Visual Basic, and creating websites (using ColdFusion, HTML, and JavaScript). Wright-Porto has also worked at NYU School of Medicine as a senior database developer for more than 8 years. In November 2009, with the troubled economy, her hours were reduced, which allowed her the opportunity to concentrate on expanding her Blogs by Heather business (`www.BlogsByHeather.com`), begin writing this book (in 2010), as well as raise her young family, Luke and Michaela.

As a creative outlet and for her love of art, she became a Stampin' Up! Demonstrator in October 2006. She is what is considered a "hobby" demonstrator, but enjoys making handmade cards for local shops, and holding classes at her home with customers, friends and family.

She is easy going, but very ambitious and detailed-oriented (how does that combination work)? She tries her best at all she does professionally and personally, gets great enjoyment in helping others and more so in making people smile. She is blessed and fortunate to have the life she has, and to be surrounded by a loving family and wonderful people.

About the Technical Reviewer

■ **Sonny Discini**, CISSP, Senior Network Security Engineer for the Montgomery County Government, Maryland, is responsible for providing support for security/technology initiatives for the Department of Technology Services along with state and federal partners.

Mr. Discini has over 17 years of Information Technology experience with 15 of those years focused primarily on IT Security. He joined the County in 2002. As a Senior Security Engineer, he is responsible for all aspects of County IT Security, including regulatory compliance, computer forensics, vulnerability and threat management, international research partnerships and enterprise architecture review and recommendation. His IT Security designs have won several awards and recognitions including the National Association of Counties (NACo) Achievement Awards for two consecutive years. Other secure systems he designed are used in correctional facilities in the state of Maryland and Florida. Prior to joining the County, Mr. Discini was a Senior Support/QA Engineer for VONE Corporation providing IT security support, solutions, and incident response for Federal, Commercial, DoD, and Educational customers.

Mr. Discini is an information security enthusiast and has spoken/presented at several IT Security forums. He publishes a monthly article on Information Security topics and often consults with authors of IT security books. Mr. Discini holds a Bachelors Degree in Computer Information Systems and Corporate Finance from St. Thomas Aquinas College.

Acknowledgments

I offer many thanks to Steve Anglin, Lead Director, for approaching me about writing this book! Much thanks to Sonny Discini, the Technical Reviewer who had the task of reading and proofing all the code and exercises throughout the book. A special thanks to Laurin Becker who did a wonderful job keeping me on schedule, offering assistance, encouragement and continued support during the entire process, start to finish. I greatly appreciate all the comments, advice, and hard work of Devleopment Editor Brian MacDonald, as well as Dominic Shakeshaft, Editorial Director. Also the Copy Editor, Chris Marcheso, Compositor, Kimberly Burton, the formatters, art team, and all of those responsible in the production of my first book. I am very grateful. Thank you all.

CHAPTER 1

■■■

Introduction

If you have searched the Web, chances are you have visited a blog—a personal or business website in which the author posts information including text, photos, videos, or audio recordings, and may also display gadgets like a visitor counter, slideshow, or related ads.

This book is written for individuals wanting to start a personal blog to share family photos; record a personal journey; blog about their business; or use a blog as another business tool to inform customers about specials, services they offer, showcase their products or services, or share tips and expertise in their business field.

The application you will be using to create your new blog is Google Blogger. It is one of the most popular and easy-to-use blog platforms. In just a few steps, you can create a blog and be on your way! Blogger makes it easy to begin blogging and quickly create an online presence, whether for business or personal use.

Why Use Google Blogger

There are a few popular blogging platforms including Blogger, Typepad, and WordPress. So why use Google Blogger? The number-one answer is because it is free. In addition, it is easy to learn and user-friendly.

Typepad requires you to purchase an unlimited package (US $14.95 a month) to be able to install a custom background and have full customization control. WordPress.com charges US $15 a year for a CSS (Cascade Style Sheet) upgrade. But Blogger allows you to customize your banner, background, posts, and footers (just about any aspect of your blog) for free. You have complete control of your blog, its elements, and functionality.

Google Blogger is a user-friendly blogging platform with all the bells and whistles. What more could you ask for?

About This Book

Beginning Google Blogger is an easy-to-read, how-to book about Blogger, loaded with step-by-step instruction and visual aids detailing many aspects of creating and managing a Blogger blog. You will learn basic concepts and advanced techniques, from creating a new blog and selecting fonts and colors to converting the blog to a three-column layout and installing custom blog graphics. You will also learn how to set up a domain name and create a navigational bar.

The journey will be fun, challenging, and keep you involved with exercises, practical applications of the most popular gadgets, search engine optimization tips, how to make money using your blog, and taking your Blogger blog beyond the basics.

The following topics will be covered throughout this book:

- Creating a new blog and publishing posts

- Designing a blog, changing its layout, and installing gadgets

- Making money and driving traffic to your blog

- Incorporating social networking tools and search engine optimization tips

- Using a domain instead of the default "BlogSpot" address

- Creating a gallery and knowing how and where to store images online

- Using advanced blog design techniques (HTML and CSS) and customization

- Developing an online store using Blogger pages

- Finding additional help and troubleshooting the most common mistakes

Starting a Blog

To begin, you will create a new Blogger blog; review and navigate the Dashboard; and learn how to create, edit, delete, and schedule posts. Posts are the substance of a blog and should be regularly published, not only to keep your readers interested in following your blog but to help improve your online ranking. Use labels to categorize blog content and allow visitors to quickly find what they are looking for. A Google Search Box can also be added to assist visitors in searching your site.

Once your blog is setup, add a personal touch by adding a theme, adjusting fonts and colors, and adding desired gadgets (sidebar items), as well as learn how to install a custom banner.

You may customize your blog's settings, such as inputting your e-mail address to review comments, modifying the Blog Description, adding HTML to put your signature at the end of each new post, or setting up a custom domain.

It is important to design your blog with your audience and purpose in mind, and then incorporate that into the blog layout, color scheme, and overall \functionality.

Make Your Blog Work For You

Continuing with the blog layout, you will learn about many gadgets Blogger has to offer, as well as additional gadgets that can be added to your site to help drive traffic to your blog (or those that are just for fun or informational). For example, it is a good idea to add a visitor counter to track visitors coming to your blog and learning about their activity.

It is also important to setup an area allowing visitors to subscribe to your blog so they can remain updated whenever you post new content.

Furthermore, you'll learn how to make money with your blog. One of the most popular methods is by using Google AdSense. Blogger has a "Monetize" area of the Dashboard specifically to work with Google AdSense. Many bloggers also add affiliate links to their sidebars where you can make money from referring others to a service or product you personally use, like, and recommend.

There are many tips that can help improve your blog's search engine ranking, from creating effective posts to paying another specialized company to handle submitting your site to search engines on a monthly basis. In this book, you will learn how adding certain gadgets to your blog can improve your ranking and broaden your online presence.

The use of social networking applications like Facebook and Twitter has become imperative for successful blogs. Like a blog, they have also become a "must have" tool and should be integrated into your blogging practices. While maintaining social networking sites (in addition to your blog) takes time, it is well worth the exposure, leads, and additional traffic they can bring to your blog, especially if it is business orientated.

Lastly, you may want to consider purchasing a domain name instead of using the "BlogSpot" address. For example, you would purchase `www.JaneDoe.com` instead of publicizing and using the default Blogger address of janedoe.blogspot.com.

Using and Storing Images

When you insert images into your Blogger blog, they are automatically stored to a Picasa Web Album. You may also create and link to additional albums. However, when adding an image to separate your blog posts, a custom banner or background, you may not want them added to your gallery and included with other graphics posted to your blog. Instead, we'll review how to use Google Sites to store, manage, and use images.

Customization

First, you will learn how to convert your Blogger template to a three-column layout, set a static background using a custom image, as well as install a post separator or footer (an image to separate each post in your blog), and modify other elements of your blog's design. In addition, you may install a type of navigational bar. This book will review how to install a textual menu that sits under your banner.

Setting Up a Blog Store

Yes, you can setup an online store using a blog. You will be using Blogger's "Pages" feature to setup a couple of pages containing items for sale or services you offer, then add payment buttons from Google Checkout and PayPal to allow customers to pay you instantly online.

Additional Resources and Help

Toward the end of this book, we'll review the most common mistakes and how they should be addressed. In addition, you will find many references to helpful Blogger and blogging sites including how to improve your blog, search engine optimization tips, HTML help, and more.

Summary

Blogging shouldn't be difficult. Google Blogger keeps it simple. Use this book to guide you step by step from the basics to more advanced blogging concepts. Most importantly, learn how to make your blog work for you to achieve your personal or professional blogging goals.

CHAPTER 2

■ ■ ■

Getting Started

Now that you know a little more about what a blog entails, it's time for you to get your hands dirty and get started. We'll begin with creating a new blog, and then review different areas of your blog and what you see on the main screen (called the Dashboard). You will also create your first post.

To begin, create a new Blogger blog. This involves creating a new Google account or using an existing one, setting your blog's title and address (your Blogspot address), and choosing a template. Next, you'll review and navigate the Dashboard and learn how to setup your profile, upload your picture, look at blog settings, and view the blog's layout and design.

Lastly, you'll learn how to create, edit, delete, and schedule posts, and view your blog to verify what your readers will see. At the end of the chapter, you should know how to navigate to different areas of your blog, although each section will be covered in greater detail throughout this book.

Creating a Blog

The first step in creating a blog is to create a name. Although Blogger allows you to change your blog's address once it is setup, it is important to take time to think about a name before getting started. The name of your blog should be related to the purpose of your blog, whether it's a personal blog about yourself in general, goals you have accomplished, a journey you are on, or a professional blog about a service or product you provide. If you were blogging about yourself, you may use your name as the blog name (and therefore part of your blog address). For example, if your name was "Jane Doe" and you used that as the name of your blog, then Blogger would assign your blog address as `janedoe.blogspot.com`. If your blog is about your landscaping company and services it provides, you could use your company name or slogan. The example we will be using throughout this book is a fictitious company called "The Perfect Landscape" with the blog address `theperfectlandcape.blogspot.com`. Once you have decided on a name, it's time to create your Google Blogger blog.

Exercise —Create a New Blog

In this exercise, you will be creating a new Blogger blog:

1. With your Internet browser open, visit `blogger.com`.

2. You will come to Blogger's home page (see Figure 2-1).

Figure 2-1. Blogger's web site

3. Click the Create a Blog button.

4. On the next screen create a new Google account (see Figure 2-2).

Figure 2-2. Google Account creation

■ **Note:** If you already have a Google account, go back to Blogger's home page and enter your Google username and password at the top right area of the screen labeled "Sign in to use Blogger with your Google account." Click Sign In.

---

5. Start with entering an e-mail address and re-type it to verify there are no typos.

6. Enter a password of at least eight characters (you will have to also do this twice). It is good practice to enter a password that contains upper and lowercase letters, punctuation marks, as well as numbers, or create an acronym. This would make it more difficult for an unauthorized user to access your blog. For example, it would not be a good idea to use your name as your password unless garbled. After you are finished typing your potential password, Google will display your password strength, such as weak, fair, good, or strong. Keep experimenting until you enter a strong password.

7. Enter a display name and birthday.

8. Enter the characters in the Word Verification box. Don't worry if you get it wrong on the first try: The letters and words are meant to be difficult to read. Google Blogger is using CAPTCHA (Completely Automated Public Turing test to tell Computers and Humans Apart), a program used to generate distorted and twisted characters for you to type in. A human can pass this sort of test, a computer could not. CAPTCHA is primarily used to help prevent spam on your blog (or web site).

9. Check the Acceptance of Terms and click Continue.

10. On the next screen, enter a Blog Name and the URL as (see Figure 2-3). Click Check Availability and if the name you chose is already taken, keep trying until you find an available one and still suits your interests.

Figure 2-3. Name your blog

11. Continue with choosing a Template. We will be reviewing the Template Designer in Chapter 3, however for now choose Picture Window.

12. Click Continue.

13. You have now created your first blog.

14. You will receive an e-mail from Google to verify your account creation. Make sure you verify your Google Blogger account by clicking the link provided in the email. You will have limited functionality until your account is verified.

Now that you have completed setting up your new blog account, click the Start Blogging button, which will bring you right into posting and the New Post area. However, we will not create a post just yet. Instead, we'll review the elements of your screen (the Dashboard) which is what you will typically see when you log into Blogger. Afterward, we will review how to create, edit, delete, and schedule posts.

Reviewing the Dashboard

From the New Post area, click Dashboard in the upper right corner of your screen. The Dashboard serves as a menu, or a way for you to navigate to different areas of your blog depending on the task at hand (see Figure 2-4). We will briefly review each option (listed below), while other areas will be discussed in more detail later in the book.

1. Profile

2. View Blog

3. New Post

4. Edit Posts

5. Settings

6. Design

7. Monetize

8. Reading list

9. Other stuff

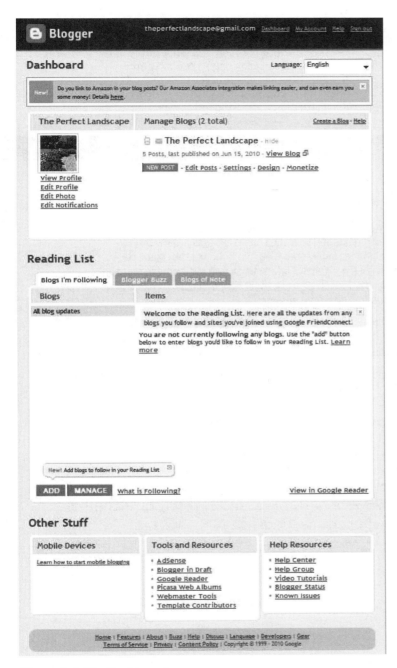

Figure 2-4. The Dashboard

Profile

This section is the area where you enter information about yourself and what information you would like to share with readers of your blog (like a traditional "About Me" page). You may enter information including your name, email address, birthday, sex, physical location (city, state, and country), interests, and mini biography. There is also a place to upload your picture. This profile image will be shown on your blog's sidebar (when inserting the Profile gadget).

Exercise—Edit Profile

Editing your profile:

1. From the Dashboard on the left side of the screen, click the Edit Profile link.

2. In this screen, enter as much or as little information about yourself that you would like to share with your blog readers. Typically, I check off to share my profile, email address, display name (normally your blog title), photograph, home page URL, location, and sometimes my general interests. Due to the increased amount of Internet fraud and security issues, be wary about how much personal information you would like to share with strangers.

3. To upload a photograph to use as your profile image, click the Browse button to locate a picture on your computer or enter a web address (URL) if using a picture from your personal online image storage site, such as Photobucket or Flickr.

4. When you have finished editing the profile, click the Save button.

5. You are back at the Dashboard.

■ **Note:** Although we have created one blog so far, creating more than one blog under this Google account will result in a list of all the blogs in the Dashboard, and all have the following options beneath them (View Blog, New Post, Edit Posts, Settings, Design and Monetize) where each pertains to the blog selected. In our example, The Perfect Landscape is the blog listed in the Dashboard (see Figure 2-4).

View Blog

Click the View Blog link to open and view your blog in an Internet browser window (see Figure 2-5).

Figure 2-5. View blog

New Post

When clicking New Post from the Dashboard, a screen appears where you can begin entering a new post. Although we will be creating a new post later in this chapter, in general you will enter a title and begin writing content in the large text box, categorize your posts by entering what Blogger calls Labels, and click Publish Post. It is then viewable to your blog readers.

Settings

In this section of the Dashboard, you can setup formatting preferences, general date/time formats, how your blog archives posts, manage comment settings, or setup a custom name (in the form of `<domain-name-here>.com` such as `ThePerfectLandscape.com`.

In addition, you can setup your blog to be protected in the sense that you invite those readers that are allowed to view your blog. You may also configure mobile settings so you may post from your mobile phone or email.

Among all the settings (many which to be reviewed throughout this book), Comments should be setup first. This is so you can start receiving notifications when people leave comments on your blog, cut down on spam-related comments by enabling Word Verification, and allow anyone to comment.

Exercise—Configure Comments Settings

From the Dashboard, click Settings and Comments and continue using these steps:

1. Under Who Can Comment, select Anyone.

2. Make sure Show Word Verification for Comments is set to Yes.

3. Enter your e-mail address in the Comment Notification e-mail section.

4. If you find you are getting many negative or spam-like comments, come back to these settings and turn on Comment Moderation. This allows you to review the comments first and decide whether you would like to publish them.

5. Click Save Settings.

Another setting that should be chosen (and may help in creating posts) is Updated Editor. While in Settings, go to the Basic tab, scroll to the bottom under Global, and click Updated Editor. Click Latest Features to review in detail all the new and improved features. The reason I mention setting this option now because of the new image handling functionality. Many people in forums have had difficulty inserting images where they would like. You can now do this easily and still have the ability to drag and drop. We will review how to insert an image when we create a new post in the next exercise.

Design

This is where you can have some fun in designing your blog. Using the Template Designer you can choose different colors for certain elements of your blog as well as which fonts to use (from the selection available), insert a background image, modify the layout of your blog (placement of your sidebars), and adjust column widths.

You may also drag and drop page elements. You do this in the Page Elements option and you can add sidebar items for your blog (Add a Gadget) including a visitor counter, slideshow, picture, links to other blogs, and web sites you like.

In the Edit HTML area is where much design and layout customization occurs. It is also in this section where you have full control of your blog's layout and design; where you can convert a two-column blog to a three-column format; and where you adjust spacing and margins, colors and borders, and more using CSS code.

When creating your blog earlier in this chapter, you chose a template for your blog (I chose Picture Window for The Perfect Landscape example). You can change your template at any time through the Template Designer.

Monetize

Blogger has a built-in feature to quickly add Google AdSense to your blog. In brief, Google AdSense adds content-related ads to your blog in the sidebar or under posts. This will be discussed further in Chapter 4.

Reading Lists

When you visit other Blogger blogs, you can choose to become a "follower" (a form of subscribing to another Blogger blog which we will discuss in Chapter 4). Those blogs appear in this section under Blogs I'm Following. There are no more steps needed to accomplish this.

This section is more informational and designed for you to read what's new with the blogs you are following with Blogger, including other noteworthy blogs.

Other Stuff

In this area of the Dashboard, you will find links to Blogger help, tools and resources like AdSense and Picasa Web Albums (two tools you will learn more about in later chapters).

Posts

Posting is what blogging is all about. Posts make up the majority of your blog and are why readers will subscribe to your blog or keep coming back to see what's new. A post can consist of a picture or many pictures, text, video, and more.

Another important area you want to include in the majority of your posts is "Labels." In Chapter 4, you will learn more about making the most of your posts, but for now think of labels as a way to group your posts and at the same time giving your readers a way to search your blog. When visitors come to your blog, you don't want them to scroll through all posts to find an area of interest. This is why you categorize your posts using labels. In our example with The Perfect Landscape, if a visitor wanted to see all posts that were tips on how to better landscape, they would click "Landscaping Tips" and only those posts with that label would be filtered and displayed for the reader.

Exercise—Creating a Post

It is finally time to create your first post:

1. From the Dashboard, click New Post. If you are currently viewing your blog, in the upper right corner click New Post.

2. From the New Post area (see Figure 2-6), enter a Title. Enter text that best describes the content of your post, and keep it brief. For this example, enter "We're Online!"

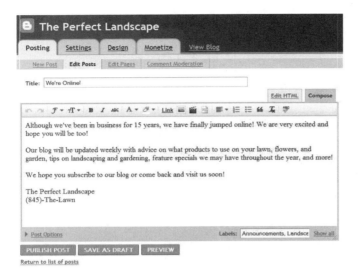

Figure 2-6. *Create a new post*

3. The large text box is where you can begin entering text. For example, type "Welcome to my blog" and write a little more about yourself or your company, and what you plan to bring readers—tips, advice, products for sale, a service, etc. In The Perfect Landscape, a brief "We're Online" was used (see Figure 2-6).

4. In the Labels for This Post, enter the words "Announcements, Landscaping Tips" to categorize this post. Notice the use of two words or phrases separated by a comma. You can assign more than one label to a post.

5. Click Publish Post if you want to publish the post immediately. You may also click Post Options, and under Labels on the right you will see Post Date and Time. That area is used to schedule a post to be published at a future date and time (for example, you would do this if you are going on vacation but want to prepare posts ahead of time and schedule them to be delivered while you're away).

6. If you want to save the post as a draft and not publish it, click Save Now and click to create a new post or other area of your blog, and it will be saved as a draft. You may need to save a post as a draft if you need to research more information or if the post is not completed.

7. Click View Post to view your new post as your readers would see it (see Figure 2-7).

■ **Note:** Labels are used to categorize your posts which allow your readers to quickly find posts of interest without having to search through your entire blog.

You should post often, but also be realistic in determining how often to post. Most of us cannot post every day, but to keep your readers interested in your blog you should post on a regular basis with relevant content to your blog's purpose, service, or theme. In our "The Perfect Landscape" example, you would post about landscaping, tips on products to use to keep your lawn green and reduce the amount of weeds, and promote services you offer or specials you are running. For example, you would not post about a Tylenol or Fisher Price product recall that you heard about on the news. That would not be relevant to landscaping.

Figure 2-7. View post

In the last exercise, you created a post, published it, and chose to view it. When viewing your blog while logged in, you will notice the small wrenches around your blog (see Figure 2-7). These will not be seen when you are logged out. Typically, many applications use a pencil to symbolize editing. Blogger uses wrenches. While you are logged in and viewing your blog, you can click any wrench to quickly and easily edit that particular area of your blog. The most popular elements in your blog are called gadgets. They can be in the form of a links list, a picture, a slideshow, a counter, or a banner, to name a few.

Also notice the Post a Comment area. This is where readers will post a comment on your post, and this box is not seen on the main blog when a reader first comes to your blog. You only see this area when a reader selects a specific post by clicking the title of the post (if this is how the Comments settings are configured).

In viewing your post, notice there are default gadgets (or elements) already setup and appearing in your sidebar (including About Me, Followers, and Archives).

In the next chapter we'll review many popular gadgets, how to add them, move them around, and remove them.

Now that you have learned how to create, publish, and view a post, in the next exercise you will learn how to edit a post and how to delete it.

Exercise—Editing a Post

In this exercise you will learn how to edit a post and insert an image:

1. From the Dashboard, click Edit Posts (see Figure 2-8) and you will see a list of all your posts (at this time, you have only created one). If you are still viewing your blog, click the Back button in your browser, then click on Dashboard from the top right.

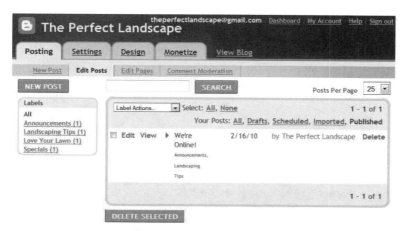

Figure 2-8. Edit posts

2. Notice that you can sort and find posts by their "status" or All, Drafts, Scheduled, Imported, or Published. Also note how many posts are given the different Labels listed on the left side.

3. On the post "We're Online!" (or whatever title you had given your post), click Edit to the left to open the post again.

4. Click the Insert Image icon on the toolbar to insert a picture. It is the third icon from the left.

5. Click Browse to upload an image from your computer (see Figure 2-9). Locate the picture you would like to upload. You will be returned to this screen with a small picture preview. Click OK to insert the image. Note that you can also upload an online image using a web address.

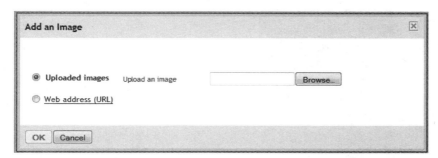

Figure 2-9. Insert image

6. Once inserted, place your mouse pointer over the image and a small menu appears (see Figure 2-10) where you can change the size of your image, align it, or remove it.

Figure 2-10. Formatting text

7. Click Publish Post.

8. If you would like, click View Post again to see how it now looks. I advise doing this so you know how your readers see your posts.

In addition to editing a post by inserting images (or other media), you may also format text including changing the font, font size, color and alignment, inserting a hyperlink, and more (see Figure 2-10). Place your mouse pointer over any toolbar icon to see the tool tip (name of the item such as the "B" for Bold). Many of these tools are identical to those used in common word processors like Microsoft Word and are applied the same way by selecting specific text.

■ **Note:** Popular keyboard shortcuts also work in Blogger's post editor, including CTRL + B for bold and CTRL + I for italic (where CTRL is the control key on your keyboard).

Exercise—Formatting a Post

Let's review some basic formatting techniques:

- If you want to format a piece of text like "The Perfect Landscape" in the previous example (see Figure 2-10), first select the words "The Perfect Landscape" and click Bold, click the Font Color icon and choose a green, and choose the Center justification tool.

- If you want to create a hyperlink, select a word or phrase, click Link (blue hyperlink), and enter the URL to the web page in which you would like to link.

- To begin a numbered or bulleted list, go to a blank line and click the desired formatting tool and begin typing. When you hit the ENTER key on the keyboard, it will automatically insert the next number or an additional bullet.

- Before posting, it is a good idea to click the Check Spelling. It will highlight the misspelled words in yellow where you can then click those words for suggestions. When finished, click Done Spellchecking.

- After formatting, continue creating the rest of your post, and publish or save as draft (see Figure 2-11 for a final view of the post).

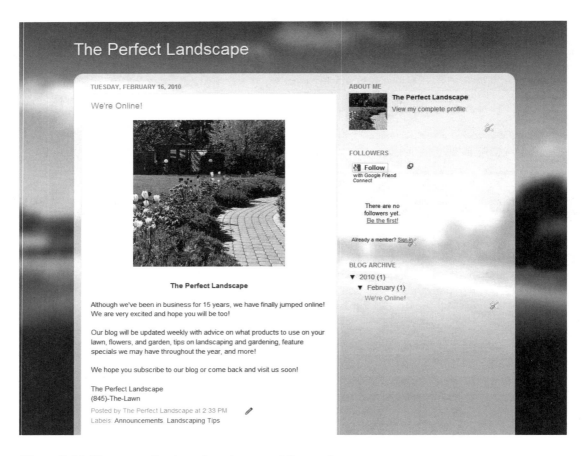

Figure 2-11. View post after inserting picture and formatting text

There may be occasions when you need to delete a post. You may do this if a promotion you were running is no longer active or the post content is no longer relevant. If you are unsure about deleting a post, set it back to draft status (drafts do not appear on your blog).

When you are finished working in your blog, remember to sign out. You don't want your readers to see all the wrenches appearing while you are working on your blog and while you are logged in.

Exercise—Deleting a Post

1. From the Dashboard, click Edit Posts (see Figure 2-8).

2. To delete the "We're Online!" post, look to the right side and click Delete. Confirm the deletion.

3. If you needed to delete multiple posts, you can check them off using the check boxes to the left of each post you want to delete.

4. Click the Delete button at the bottom and again confirm the deletion.

Summary

In this chapter, you learned how to create a blog, reviewed the Dashboard and each of the elements within the Dashboard (Edit Profile, View Blog, New Post, Edit Posts, Settings, Design, and Monetize), and the different options within each item including how to set up comments and where to find the Template Designer to adjust the fonts, colors, background, and layout of your blog.

Through exercises in this chapter, you also learned how to create, edit, format, and delete a post; in addition, how to schedule a post and set it to a draft or publish it for your readers to see. You should view a post after it is published to be sure it is formatted the way you intended and how you would like it displayed to your readers.

Posting is the heart of blogging. It is important that you post often and that each post contains relevant content—information pertaining to the blog's purpose. In the next chapter you will learn more about your blog's layout and design, while in this chapter we covered the basics to get started. Congratulations on creating your new blog!

■ ■ ■

CHAPTER 3

Blog Layout and Design

Blog layout and design is one area many bloggers enjoy and look forward to. It is here you can show personality and have fun experimenting with different settings. You will be using the Template Designer to choose a different template for your blog, set the main color scheme, choose a layout and background, as well as customize specific page elements, such as the color and font of post titles, page text, link color and more.

You will also learn how to add gadgets like a calendar or search box, as well as remove, or rearrange gadgets in your blog's sidebar. In the header area of your blog's layout, you will be installing a custom banner to use in addition to the desired Blogger template.

Although we'll review Page Elements and Template Designer in the Design area of your blog, you will learn how to further customize your blog using HTML and CSS code in Chapter 7, within the Edit HTML area.

Page Elements

When entering the Design portion of your blog from the Dashboard, you will see three tabs: Page Elements, Edit HTML, and Template Designer. Page Elements displays a visual layout of your blog and where all your gadgets lie. A gadget is an item in your blog's layout. When you first created your blog in Chapter 2, there were gadgets that Blogger automatically inserted into your blog's layout (see Figure 3-1): About Me, Followers, Archives, and Page Header (the banner area which currently displays your Blog's Title and Description previously entered in Chapter 2). Gadgets can be deleted at any time. We discuss gadgets in more detail later in this chapter.

In addition to the existing gadgets in your layout, there are other elements or areas of your blog that we'll review, such as the Navbar, Header, Blog Posts, and gadgets like a Search Box.

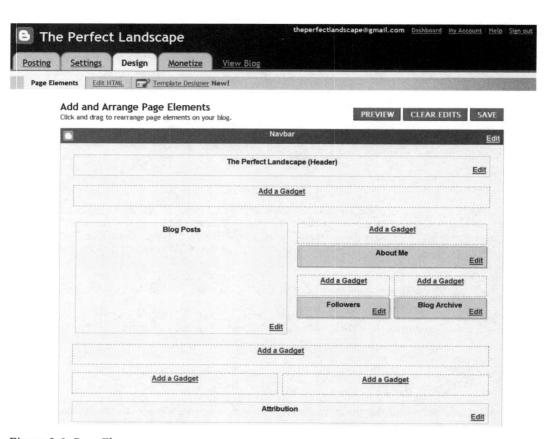

Figure 3-1. *Page Elements*

Navbar

The Navbar is a built-in feature of your blog used to quickly navigate to your Design, compose a New Post, or to Sign Out, and displays your email (username). On the left side on the Navbar when viewing your blog, you will also see an area to report abuse, or the ability to go to the next Blogger blog.

In the Navbar page element, you can edit the Navbar color to best match the coloring of your blog. The only option when editing the Navbar (without using custom HTML/CSS code) is choosing a color. I would recommend one of the "transparent" settings (see Figure 3-2).

Exercise – Editing the Navbar

Choose a transparent color for your blog's Navbar:

1. From the Dashboard, choose Design.

2. Click Page Elements if not already selected.

3. On the Navbar, click Edit.

4. From the options shown in Figure 3-2, choose Transparent Dark or Transparent Light or any other available color that best compliments your blog. In The Perfect Landscape's blog, Transparent Dark was chosen.

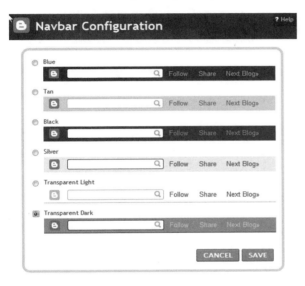

Figure 3-2. Navbar Configuration

5. Click Save.

6. Choose View Blog to view your changes (notice your Navbar color changed).

Gadgets

In the way posts make up the majority of your blog, gadgets make up the majority of your blog's layout, particularly the sidebar(s). We will begin with basic gadgets available from Blogger when clicking Add a Gadget (see Figure 3-3). In the next chapter and throughout the remainder of this book, you learn how to add additional third-party gadgets to promote your blog, connect to popular social networking sites, make money, or further customize the design or functionality of your blog.

Figure 3-3. Add a Gadget

■ **Note:** Gadgets are primarily added to your blog's sidebar for quick, visual access.

Let's review a list of commonly used gadgets (see Table 3-1) and then add a few popular gadgets to your blog, such as a Search Box, in the following exercises. You do not want to clutter your sidebar(s) making your blog appear too busy, nor will every gadget suit your blog's purpose or appeal to all blog readers. Pick and choose those that you need and from which you will benefit.

Table 3-1: Basic Gadgets Review

Gadget	Description
Pages	Allows you to create content on your blog separate from your main post area. It is similar to the traditional web page describing a service you may offer, list products you sell, or a custom About Me or About Us page (this feature will be reviewed in Chapter 8 in setting up an online/blog store).
Followers	Displays a list of people following your blog (in their Dashboard under Other Blogs, it will show your blog updates).
Search Box	Adds a Google Search box to your blog allowing visitors to quickly and easily search your blog.
HTML/JavaScript	Primarily used to add third-party gadgets to your blog.
AdSense	Provides capability to earn money with your blog by adding Google AdSense.
Picture	Use this gadget to add a picture to your blog's sidebar, footer, or header area (in addition to your Profile Photo). This gadget is not used to insert an image into a Post.
Slideshow	Creates a quick slideshow from Picasa Web Album, Flickr, Photobucket, or other photo storage sources.
Link List	Creates a link to your favorite blogs, web sites, photo albums, or other links.
Labels	Displays a list of categories (labels) used in your blog posts.
Subscription Links	Allows a reader to subscribe to your blog's posts or comments using popular readers like Google Reader.
Profile	Allows you to add certain profile information to your blog, including the Profile Photo if one was uploaded.
Blog Archive	Select how to archive your blog's posts; most commonly is by month.
Page Header	Add a header area to your blog. Your blog banner would typically go here.

Search Box

In the next exercise you will add a Search Box to your blog allowing readers to quickly and easily search your blog. You want to keep them on your site as long as possible, and allow them the ability to find what they need especially if you are selling product or promoting an event on your site. This gadget uses Google, which can be advantageous.

Exercise – Adding a Search Box

After blogging for a while, you will have many posts, labels (categories), and archives. Adding a Search Box allows visitors to quickly search your blog without scrolling or visiting many labels trying to locate what they are looking for. They can type in a word or phrase and click Search to get results.

1. From within Page Elements in the right sidebar (right-side column of your screen), click Add a Gadget at the top of the column.

2. From the Basics list, choose Search Box (see Figure 3-4).

Figure 3-4. Configure the Search Box gadget

3. Check "This Blog" since the purpose of the exercise is to allow visitors the ability to search your blog. However, you may also like using the search engine to search pages you've linked to or to search the Web as well. In our example, all three have been selected.

4. You can also change the Title of the gadget. The default is "Search This Blog" used in our example. Another preferable option is "Search My Blog."

5. Click Save.

6. It is now added to your sidebar, the first/top item.

7. Drag the gadget to a new location and drop (or release your mouse) in the new desired location (above Blog Archive).

8. Click Save.

9. Again and after any change in your blog's layout, click View Blog to see your changes live.

Subscription Links

The next gadget we'll review and add to your blog is the Subscription Link (Figure 3-5). This gadget allows visitors to subscribe to your posts or comments, informing them when you post to your blog or when comments are added.

Figure 3-5. Configure Subscription Links

Exercise – Adding Subscription Links

Adding this gadget allows readers to stay updated by following your blog's posts or comments:

1. From within Page Elements in the right sidebar, click Add a Gadget.

2. From the Basics list, choose Subscription Links.

3. Change the title if you would like.

4. Click Save.

5. It is now added to your sidebar, the first/top item.

6. Again and after any change in your blog's layout, click View Blog to see your changes live.

Labels

In the next example we'll add Labels. In Chapter 2, you created a new post and assigned two labels to that post. Those labels will now appear in your sidebar once the Labels gadget is added. Again, you can assign more than one label per post. As you continue creating new posts and assigning new labels, the Labels list will automatically grow in your sidebar.

Categorizing (or labeling) your posts allow visitors to quickly find posts of interest. You do not have to label every post if it's a quick note, but you should label the majority of them, and this will help with your search engine ranking (as discussed in Chapter 4).

Exercise – Adding Labels

Provide your readers with a category list on your blog so they can quickly find posts and topics of interest:

1. From within Page Elements, in the right sidebar, click Add a Gadget.

2. From the Basics list, choose Labels (see Figure 3-6).

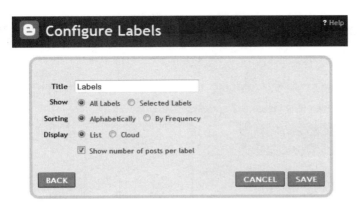

Figure 3-6. Configure Labels

3. If you would like, change the title (see Figure 3-6). You can leave it with the Title "Labels" or you can change it to "Categories" as done in The Perfect Landscape example (see Figure 3-15).

4. Keep the defaults shown in Figure 3-6.

5. Click Save.

6. It is now added to your sidebar, the first/top item in your Page Elements page.

7. Click and drag the gadget to be placed before (above) the Blog Archive gadget.

8. Click Save again to save the layout change.

9. Again and after any change in your blog's layout, click View Blog to see your changes live.

Link List

You may have other blogs or sites you often visit that you would like to share with your blog readers. For example, in The Perfect Landscape, it will contain links to other sites providing information about how to maintain your lawn, garden, patios, and overall landscape. This list is personalized and based on about the topic of your blog. This list is personalized, and it is good practice to link to sites with similar interests.

■ **Note:** Keep in mind that when your readers click on one of these links, it will open that site in the current Internet window and take focus off your blog.

Exercise – Adding a Links List

Link to and share with your readers your favorite sites or blogs:

1. From within Page Elements in the right sidebar, click Add a Gadget.

2. From the Basics list, choose Link List (see Figure 3-7 appears).

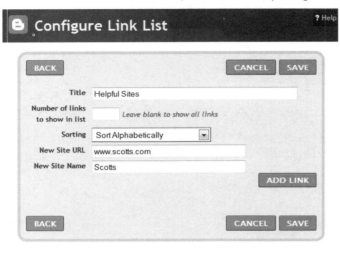

Figure 3-7. Configure Link List

3. Enter a Title (see Figure 3-7).

4. For Sorting, choose "Sort Alphabetically."

5. In New Site URL, enter the URL address of the first item to add.

6. Enter the textual name (New Site Name) you would like shown in your list (your readers don't see the full URL in the sidebar, only the name).

7. Click Add Link to add another link and again enter the URL and Site Name.

8. Continue clicking Add Link for as many links you would like to add.

9. When finished, click Save.

10. It is now added to your sidebar, the first/top item.

11. Click and drag the gadget to be placed on the bottom right.

12. Click Save again to save the layout change.

13. Again and after any change in your blog's layout, click View Blog to see your changes live.

Google Calendar

Regardless of your business or if you are creating your blog for personal use, there may be events or dates you would like to promote or share with your readers. Google Calendar is an efficient tool for this and can be configured to fit in your blog's sidebar (and this is a free tool).

Exercise – Adding Google Calendar

Google Calendar is a third-party gadget you will be adding to your blog, as it does not currently exist on the list of gadgets when you click "Add a Gadget" from within Blogger.

1. Go to google.calendar.com.

2. If necessary, re-enter your Google Account password and sign in, and the "Welcome to Google Calendar" screen is displayed.

3. Enter your First Name, Last Name, Location, and Time Zone.

4. Click Continue.

5. On the next screen you'll see your calendar (see Figure 3-8).

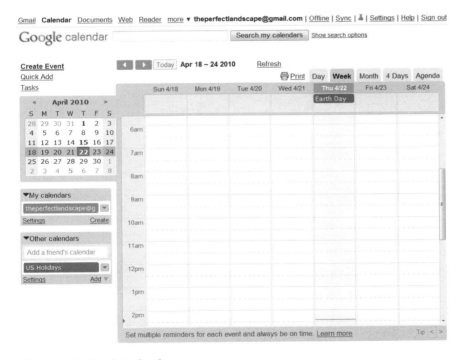

Figure 3-8. Google Calendar

6. Double-click a desired date and time and a small window appears (see Figure 3-9) with the date and time (one hour by default) and a place for you to enter the name of the event. In The Perfect Landscape Example, on April 22 (Earth Day), a demonstration at Home Depot is scheduled from 11 a.m.–4 p.m., however it only shows 11 a.m.–12 p.m. Click Edit Event Details if you need to modify the event details from the defaulted time slot settings, or Create Event if the time is what you would like.

Figure 3-9. Create New Event

7. In our example (The Perfect Landscape), click Edit Event Details (see Figure 3-10). Notice the time change, that a Description was added, and the option to set the Privacy to Public.

    a. Depending on the type of event, you can choose Private or Add Guests.

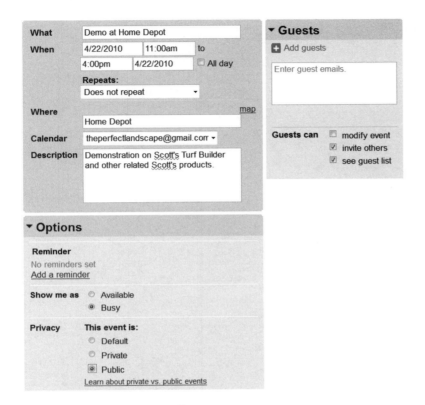

Figure 3-10. Edit Event Details

8. Click Save and the event will appear highlighted on the calendar.

9. Continue adding your events.

Now, make the entire calendar public and configure it to fit your sidebar:

10. On the left under My Calendars, click Settings.

11. Click Share This Calendar under Sharing.

12. Check off "Make the calendar public" and click Save.

13. Click Yes to confirm that you are making the calendar public.

14. Click the same area, but you'll see instead of "Share This Calendar" it says "Shared: Edit Settings."

15. Click the Calendar Details tab (see Figure 3-11).

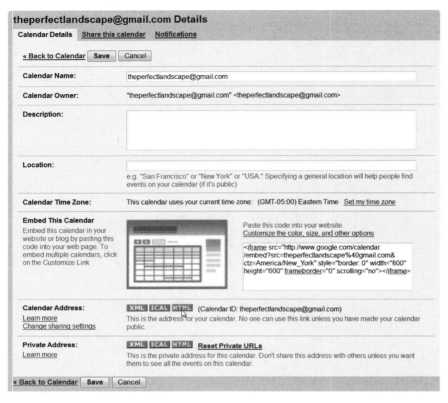

Figure 3-11. Calendar Details

16. Under Calendar Address, click HTML.

17. Click Configuration Tool.

18. Enter the settings in Figure 3-12 (enter your own Title if Upcoming Events is not what you would like).

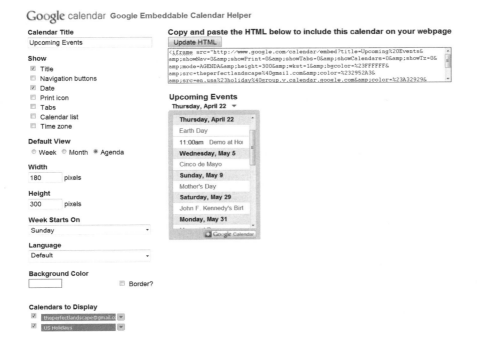

Figure 3-12. Google Embeddable Calendar Helper

b. Notice the Width is set to 180px. This is because your sidebar by default is between 180px - 220px approximately (depending on the template chosen), but in Chapter 7 we set the width to 200px, and the 180px will fit best without being truncated.

c. Make sure you select Default View as Agenda.

19. Copy all of the code in the large text box at the top of the page.

20. Go back to Blogger, go to Design, and Page Elements.

21. Click Add a Gadget and choose HTML/JavaScript.

22. Enter a title such as "Click Here to View" since you already have the word "Upcoming Events" as the title in your Google Calendar settings. Or if you would like the title to appear blank (no title), then enter a title in this form <!--Google Calendar-->. Since the Title is within the HTML Comment tags, the title will not be displayed when viewing your blog, but a title is needed to add the gadget.

23. Click Save and the gadget is added to your sidebar as the first item.

24. Drag and drop where you would like it to appear.

25. Click Save when finished.

26. Click View Blog.

Now or at any time, you can go back to Google Calendar and continue adding events and the sidebar calendar will automatically update. You do not have to add a new gadget for every event.

While we went through Google Calendar in order to have your events listed on your blog, you can visit `google.com/support/calendar/?hl=en` for more help with Google Calendar.

Install a Banner

You may have designed a banner for your new blog (Page Header) or may have one designed for you in the future. A banner is typically a graphically designed image taking the place of the text in the Page Header area (currently "The Perfect Landscape" in our example).

You may choose to have it appear behind your blog's title (if it's more of a background type of image) or instead of your blog's title and description. You may load the image from your computer or online image storage location (if you have images on Photobucket, for instance).

Exercise – Installing a Banner

In this example, you will be modifying the Page Header and upload an image to use as your blog's banner.

1. From within Page Elements next to the Header area, click Edit. The Configure Header window will appear (see Figure 3-13).

Figure 3-13. Configure Header

2. In this example for The Perfect Landscape, an image was loaded from a computer. Under the From Your Computer area, click Browse.

3. Find the desired image on your computer.

4. After it is uploaded, you will see a snapshot of the banner (see Figure 3-14).

5. Under Placement, choose Behind or Instead of title and description. Since The Perfect Landscape's banner image has text in the image, I chose Instead of title and description (see Figure 3-14).

6. Click Save.

Figure 3-14. Configure Header after image uploaded

7. After any change in your blog's layout, click View Blog to see your changes live (see Figure 3-15).

Figure 3-15. Banner installed

If your image is too large, you can go back and edit the gadget and choose "Shrink to Fit" or manually resize the image before uploading using a photo-editing program like Adobe Photoshop.

■ **Note:** In this example, the banner width is set to 930px wide.

Template Designer

You had a sneak peek at the Template Designer when setting up your blog in the last chapter, however here we will review it in more detail. The Template Designer allows you to apply a selected design to your blog, as well as permit background, layout, color and font customization. Under Advanced, you have the ability to enter CSS code (however, we discuss CSS customization and coding in Chapter 7, Advanced Blog Design).

The Template Designer is composed of the following elements:

1. Templates
2. Background
   a. Background Image.
   b. Main Color Theme.
3. Layout
   a. Body Layout.
   b. Footer Layout.
   c. Adjust Width.
4. Advanced
   a. Page elements (such as Page Text, Background, Links, Blog Title, and many more) listed where you can change the color and font.
   b. Add CSS.

Templates

Blogger has a collection of beautiful, professional templates for your blog. Under each category, there are options. For example, we chose the Picture Window template, in Templates and under Picture Window, you'll find a few different scenes. In Figure 3-16, the 2nd scenery scheme is chosen, which complements The Perfect Landscape banner design and nature theme. Click on some others and view the preview, then be sure to go back to Picture Window as we review more options in the Template Designer, Background.

Figure 3-16. Templates in Blogger Template Designer

Background

Some templates include a background image, like Picture Window, while others do not, such as Simple. However, you can apply a new background to Picture Window, or any other template in the Template Designer by selecting an image from Blogger's collection (see Figure 3-17). In the next exercise, you will choose a background image that looks like a bunch of grass, which better suits The Perfect Landscape landscaping business.

Exercise – Choose Template Background

Choose another background image to use with the selected Picture Window template (and The Perfect Landscape blog).

1. Click on Backgrounds, on the left, in the Template Designer and the list of available options for modifying your background are shown (where these options pertain to the selected Picture Window template).

2. Click the Background Image dropdown and another window will pop-up with a plentiful selection of different types of backgrounds (see Figure 3-17) from abstract to business to family to nature, and many more.

3. For this example, click Nature, then click on the grass image (second column, second row).

4. Click Done. You are back again at the Template Designer.

Figure 3-17. Backgrounds in Blogger Template Designer

From within Backgrounds, you may also change the Main Color Theme of your blog. Click the dropdown box for Main Color Theme or choose a color from the Suggested Themes palette. It will change the color of your Post Title and Links. To change the color of specific elements of your blog, like the Post Title, click on Advanced from the left sidebar of the Template Designer. We will review that area as well in upcoming exercises.

If after experimenting you want to go back to the original template settings, click on "Use default background and colors."

Layout

Under Layout, Blogger has many different forms for your blog in the Body Layout area, one of the most common being the three column layout (where there is a sidebar on the left, main area for posting in the middle, and then another sidebar on the right), but there are some others to choose from which may also suit your blogging needs. You may also choose a layout for the footer area of your blog (in the Footer Layout section).

I know personally that many people would love to change the widths of their columns without having to do it in HTML or CSS code. Well, under Adjust Width, you can do just that!

Exercise – Change Layout

In this exercise, you will choose the three column format as well as adjust the widths of the three columns.

1. Click on Layout, and then under Body Layout, click on the 1st layout in the 2nd row (the traditional three column layout form), see Figure 3-18.

2. Next, click on Adjust Widths (see Figure 3-19), and modify them as you'd like, but I left the value of 930px for the Entire Blog width since the banner for The Perfect Landscape was sized to fit the original Picture Window layout. However, notice if you modify the value of the left and right sidebar, the middle area in the preview automatically adjusts.

3. In The Perfect Landscape example, the Left Sidebar and Right Sidebar widths were set to 200px.

You can set the widths back to their original settings by clicking the Reset Widths to Template Default.

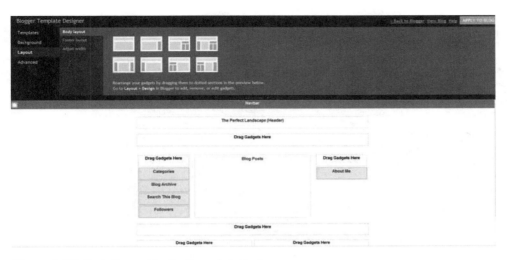

Figure 3-18. *Body Layout in the Template Designer*

Figure 3-19. *Adjust Widths in the Template Designer*

Advanced

The Advanced tab is the last stop in the Template Designer. In Advanced settings, you can modify the color and font of specific elements on your blog (such as the Page Text, Background, Links, Blog Title, Post, and much more) to better coordinate with the your new banner design. See Table 3-2 for a complete list of blog elements that you can customize.

When choosing colors, you can choose from the available color palettes or enter the six-character hexadecimal code for a desired color if you have that from a graphic designer or from a program like Adobe Photoshop.

Figure 3-20. The Advanced tab in the Template Designer

Table 3-2: List of Blog Elements

Gadget	Description
Page Text	The color of your post and sidebar text.
Backgrounds	Change the color of the background for your posts, your header, or the entire outer background (which consists of the header, sidebars, and posting areas).
Links	Set the colors for the main link color, visited link color, and hover link color (when your mouse is placed over a link, and it changes color, that is the hover link color).
Blog Title	The color and font of your Blog Title.
Tabs Text	In Chapter 8, we review how to set up a blog store and in doing so we'll create a navigational bar. In this section, Tabs Text, you can set the color and font of the text in the menu bar, as well as the font of the selected menu item.
Tabs Background	Similar to Tabs Text, however you are setting the color for the background of the navigational bar (menu bar).
Post	Set the font for your posts, as well as the footer color and border color.

Gadget	Description
Gadgets	Gadgets are your sidebar items. Here you set the font and color of the sidebar headings.
Footer	Set the font and color of items that appear in the footer area of your blog (not the same as the post footer).
Footer Links	Set the font and color of the footer links.
Add CSS	Write custom CSS code to override the existing color and font settings.

Although you have access to all these elements, you do not have to modify all or any of them. But as you are learning about Blogger and its different elements, I would suggest experimenting to see the effects and how they appear on your blog in the available Preview window. In Chapter 7 you will learn how to modify other elements of your blog's template, such as sidebar padding, borders, and background color (options not available in Advanced settings and must be done in CSS code), as well additional advanced design techniques.

Exercise – Changing Page Text Color

Have some fun experimenting with color and different elements of your site. The preview will update with your changes. You can cancel changes by clicking "clear advanced settings to <blog element>," where <blog element> represents whatever element you are currently modifying.

1. To change the color of your text to black, click on Page Text, click the dropdown box to the right of Text Color and choose black, or enter #000000 into the text box under Text Color (which currently had #333333 in The Perfect Landscape Example). The preview will update.

2. Continue experimenting with color and fonts of your choice.

When you have finished making changes to your blog design using the Template Designer, click on Apply To Blog in the upper, right corner of the Template Designer Screen (and your live blog is now updated). Continue by clicking Back to Blogger. Then view your blog to see your new design (see Figure 3-21).

Figure 3-21. *Completed Template Designer Modifications*

Summary

I hope you had fun designing your new blog and you'll continue doing so in Chapter 7. In this chapter, you added a few sidebar items including a link list of sites you would suggest your visitors to read, an area to allow readers to subscribe to your blog, a category list so readers can quickly find posts of interest, and a tool to allow users to search all content in your blog. There are hundreds of gadgets you can add to your blog, but only choose those you believe your visitors will enjoy and improve the overall function of your blog.

Up next is "Making the Most of Your Blog" where you will be adding more gadgets available in Blogger's Basics selection, as well as other popular third-party gadgets to help increase your blog's online visibility, integrate with Twitter and Facebook, track visitor activity and more.

■ ■ ■

CHAPTER 4

Making the Most of Your Blog

At this point, you have set up your blog, started entering posts, and customized its design. In this chapter, you will learn how to make your blog work for you. This chapter contains a lot of information, but it's all needed for you to make the most of your blog in whatever areas are most important to you, including:

- Increasing traffic

- Integrating social networking applications

- Tracking visitor activity

- Making money

Whether you are creating your blog for personal use or to help promote and build your business, you want to keep readers coming back. The process of increasing traffic (visits) to your blog is known as search engine optimization (SEO). The more readers visit and the more popular your blog becomes, the higher you will be listed in search engine results (known as ranking).You can easily and quickly integrate with Twitter, Facebook, and other social networking sites and increase your visibility on the Web.

In addition, you will learn ways of tracking visitor activity and use that information to better focus your marketing efforts, or to see what most interests your readers.

Lastly, with just a few clicks, you can set up Google AdSense and start making a little money by placing related ads on your site.

Increasing Traffic

Let's review a few ways to help drive traffic to your blog and keep your existing readers coming back for more. This can include setting up email subscriptions, entering appropriate post material, using meta tags, as well as adding other gadgets like AddThis, Backlinks and Blogrolls. Yes, it may seem like a lot to do, but many of these items have to only be set up once and your blog does the rest.

FeedBurner Email Subscriptions

In the last chapter, you installed the Subscription Links gadget allowing visitors to subscribe to your blog using a "reader" including the popular Google Reader. However, there are still many Internet users that don't know what a reader is or how to use it. An alternative (and popular) option is allowing your readers to subscribe via email. This means that whenever you post to your blog, the reader would get an email listing the post or posts you've recently published. Although a reader may be commonly unfamiliar, many readers know how to use email and check it often. You want to give your readers every opportunity to subscribe to your blog and stay updated with its content.

■ **Note** To learn about Google Reader, visit `reader.google.com` and take a tour.

FeedBurner is another free tool provided by Google and will allow blog visitors to subscribe to your blog via email. You will create a feed—a data format allowing your blog subscribers to stay updated with your blog's content. Once created, you may also view stats on those who have subscribed, which will be reviewed later in this section.

Although we go through all the steps in setting up your feed and adding the FeedBurner gadget to your blog, this book will not cover all aspects, tools, or functionality of FeedBurner.

Exercise—Setting Up and Installing FeedBurner

In this exercise, you will be installing an email subscription service using FeedBurner. Once the feed is created, you will get the HTML code needed to be inserted into a gadget in your blog's sidebar. Please use the following steps:

1. Log in to your Blogger account.

2. Open another Internet window and go to `feedburner.google.com`. You may have to re-enter your Google password (the password you used to login to Blogger).

In the next screen, you will create a feed for your blog (see Figure 4-1). Copy and paste your blog's address into the text box "Burn a feed right this instant." Click Next.

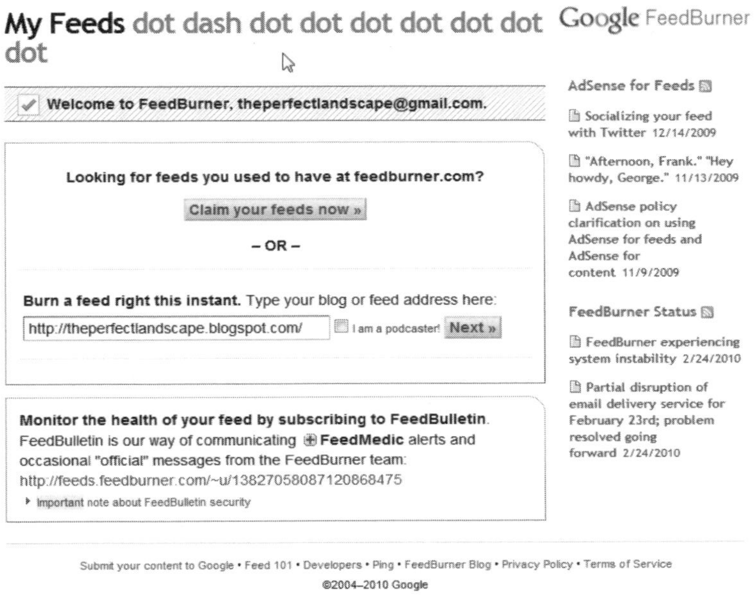

Figure 4-1. Burn a feed

3. In the next screen "Identify a Feed Source," choose either format. In this example for The Perfect Landscape, the default "Atom" was used.

4. Click Next and you are now at a screen that has generated your Feed Title and Feed Address (see Figure 4-2).

5. You may modify the Feed Title if necessary. Don't change anything in the Feed Address. Click Next.

6. Your feed has now been set up (see Figure 4-3). You may click Next to setup and review FeedBurner Stats or click "Skip directly to feed management."

Figure 4-2. Feed title and feed address

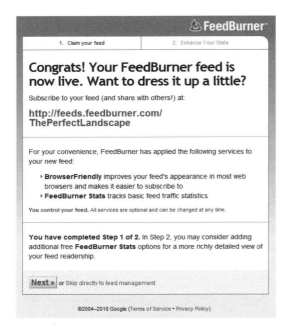

Figure 4-3. Feed setup complete

7. Let's continue setting up the Feed Stats (it's one additional step). Again, by tracking your readers' actions, you will better learn about what your readers like.

8. Using The Perfect Landscape example, Clickthroughs is checked as well as "I want more! Have FeedBurner Stats also track" (see Figure 4-4).

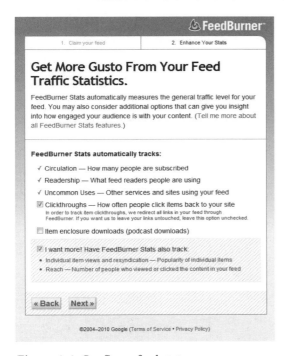

Figure 4-4. Configure feed stats

9. Click Next and you have completed the FeedBurner setup (see Figure 4-5).

Figure 4-5. Successfully updated the feed

10. In the future, if you want to review your FeedBurner statistics, click the Analyze tab. But for now, to add the gadget to your blog to allow email subscriptions, click Publicize.

11. Click Email Subscriptions (see Figure 4-6).

12. Click Activate. You only have to do this once when first setting up the Email Subscriptions.

13. Within a few seconds, you should receive a message about successfully activating the service. If you get an error, log out, log back in; go to your feed; click Publicize, Email Subscriptions, and try again.

14. Copy the code in the large text box where it states "Copy and paste the following code into any web page" (see Figure 4-6).

15. Go to Blogger and from the Dashboard go to Design and Page Elements (see Chapter 3, Figure 3-1).

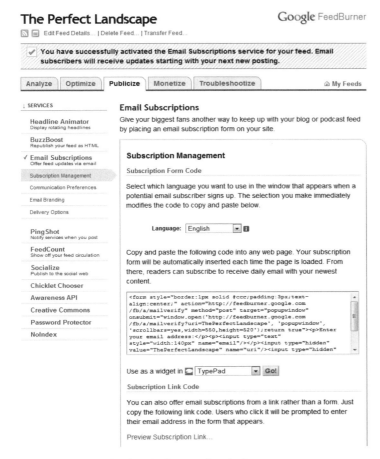

Figure 4-6. Email subscriptions, subscription management

16. Click Add a Gadget in the sidebar (as shown previously in Chapter 3, Figure 3-4).

17. Choose HTML/JavaScript.

18. In the Title, leave it blank, write "Subscribe Here," "Keep Updated," or anything else you would like.

19. Paste the HTML code from FeedBurner into the large text box (Figure 4-7).

20. Click Save.

Figure 4-7. Configure HTML/JavaScript

21. Drag and drop where you would like the gadget to appear in your sidebar. In our example with The Perfect Landscape it appears under About Me.

22. Click Save.

23. View Blog.

While this was a long exercise, it was well worth it. You have completed adding the FeedBurner Email Subscriptions, and your readers now have a choice to subscribe to your blog using a reader like Google Reader or the ability to sign up for email updates.

■ **Note** While in your FeedBurner account and Email Subscriptions, in the left sidebar under Email Subscriptions is Delivery Options. This is where you can schedule when your subscribers will receive your daily updates.

Post Content and Keywords

Now that you have installed different methods for your visitors to keep updated about your blog and to receive all posted content (Subscriptions Link from Chapter 3 and now FeedBurner), it is important to make those posts work for you. No, not every post has to be about business or promoting a service or product, and it's actually not a good idea to make every post an advertisement (or readers can easily lose interest). However, most posts should:

- Be well written

- Contain keywords about your business or personal blog topic

Since the goal is to have many people reading your blog and its content, it is good practice to make sure there are not any obvious spelling or grammatical errors. The Post Editor contains a spell checker (see Figures 2-6 and 2-10 in Chapter 2). In addition, try to keep each post focused on one particular topic, date, or event. You may lose readers if it is too "busy" or time consuming to read all the content. It is also a good idea to include keywords in your post content and post title, if possible. This will help potential customers find you on the Internet when searching for those keywords. For example, The Perfect Landscape's blog posts may include keywords or phrases "landscaping", "landscape", "lawn service", "Rockland County", "The Perfect Landscape", "waterfalls", "gazebos", "pavers" or "patios." The ultimate goal in using keywords is to have a search engine (like Google) rank your site on the first or second page of search engine results.

Although it is important to use keywords, it is also just as important to not overuse them. If you do, your site will be flagged as "spam" and will not show at all on result pages. Years ago, I downloaded free software from Apex, Dynamic Submission (`apexpacific.com/submission.html`), and at the time it stated that keywords should make up only 2 to 3 percent of your content. Out of 100 words, you should only use a keyword no more than three times.

Lastly, you should post often. Posting to your blog consistently (a few times a week) has proven to increase popularity and traffic to blogs. Your subscribers get your posts and may forward them to friends, who then may subscribe to or visit your blog. Visitors may comment on your blog posts or link to them from their site, or they may use the social networking share buttons (like the AddThis feature described later in this chapter) to share your information with their Facebook fans, Twitter followers, or MySpace friends. As you can see, a post may travel far and be seen by many.

Meta Tags

A meta tag is a line of HTML code describing your site. Traditionally, you would place meta tags at the top of every web page; one for keywords, another for description. Although they would not be seen by viewers of your web page, they would be used by search engines (such as Google). It would appear in this form (in using The Perfect Landscape example):

```
<HEAD>
<TITLE>The Perfect Landscape.</TITLE>
<META name ="description" content="The Perfect Landscape is a full-service landscape ↵
company providing lawn and garden maintenance, paver walkways and driveways, masonry work,↵
 gazebos, and waterfalls.">
<META name ="keywords" content="The Perfect Landscape, landscape, landscaping, landscape↵
 design, pavers, gazebos, waterfalls">
</HEAD>
```

Keywords are those that best describe your business or blog's purpose. The description contains your keywords, but in sentence style. If someone used Google to search for one of your keywords (for example "landscaping") and you were listed on the search results page, the meta description would appear under your listing providing the user with a brief summary of your business.

However, because so many people abused meta keywords, many search engines don't use the meta tags in their algorithms anymore. But it doesn't hurt to include them on your blog.

Exercise—Adding META Tags

In this exercise, you will add meta tags to your blog:

1. From the Dashboard, go to Design, Edit HTML.

2. Scroll down to find the HTML code "<head>".

3. Enter the following code, but replace with keywords and descriptions that best suit your blogging needs:

```
<head>
<meta name="keywords" content="landcaping, landscape, the perfect landscape, rockland
county, lawn service, gazebos, patios, waterfalls" />
<meta name="description" content="The Perfect Landscape is the landscape company to call
if you need professional lawn service, gardnering, landscaping. We also design and
install custom gazebos, patios and waterfalls." />
```

4. Click Save.

Blog Title and Description

When you first created your Blogger blog during the setup in Chapter 1, you were asked to enter a Title. However, you should also go to Settings and enter a description. In the description, enter the same or similar text you wrote in the meta description tag above. Use keywords that will help people find you on the Internet as much as possible (in post titles and content, in naming images, etc.).

Backlinks

A Backlink is similar to someone creating a traditional hyperlink back to your blog, and in fact, that is what the majority of readers still do. Backlinks have to do with linking to a specific post rather than the main blog itself. In enabling Backlinks, you can see who is linking back to a specific post on your blog, see a snippet of their post containing your link, and a link to their blog.

Exercise—Setting Backlinks

1. From the Dashboard, go to Settings, Comments.

2. Next to Backlinks, click Show.

3. Click Save Settings. At the bottom of each post (near Comments) you will see "Links to this Post." When clicked, this will list blog posts linking to your blog's post.

Blogrolls

Similar to a list of links to blogs you like, a Blog List (more commonly known as a Blogroll) is an active, live, or visual link to another blog. It contains more than just a text link; it shows a snippet of the author's most recent post (image and text or just text if no image was posted). Blogrolls can be used to increase traffic to your blog. Although your Blogroll is a list of other people's blogs, typically the link is reciprocated: it's considered good blog etiquette. However, do not be offended if someone you have linked to prefers not to link back to your site. It may be that company policy prevents them from doing so without prior authorization.

So, how does it help your ranking? The more Blogrolls you are listed on the greater the possibility that visitors of their blogs will click on a link to your blog (since the Blogroll displays a snippet of your recent blog post). In addition, the more incoming links (links or traffic directed from other sites to your blog) you have to your blog, the better your ranking will be.

Exercise—Adding a Blogroll

After you have created your Blogroll (or even before you create it), contact the bloggers you are linking to and ask if they have a Blogroll on their site or if they can link back to you:

1. From the Dashboard, go to Design, Page Elements, and Add a Gadget.

2. Choose Blog List (see Figure 4-8).

Figure 4-8. Configure blog list

3. Check to include "Snippet of most recent item" and "Thumbnail of most recent item." This shows a live or visual representation of the blogs you are linking to in your Blog List.

4. Click Add to List to add your first site (see Figure 4-9).

Figure 4-9. Add to your blog list

5. Add the URL of the site and click Add.

6. Click Add to List for each blog you would like to add. You will see the list grow in the Configure Blog List screen.

7. When finished, click Save.

8. Drag and drop where you would like the list in your sidebar.

9. Click Save to save changes.

10. Click View Blog to view your new list.

AddThis Gadget

Another way to increase your blog's popularity is giving readers the ability to quickly and easily share your posts. AddThis is a popular tool to accomplish this. With this gadget, your blog readers can share your blog's content using Facebook, Twitter, MySpace, Digg, Delicious, Google, and more.

Exercise—Installing and Adding AddThis

By allowing visitors to share your content, you increase traffic to your blog:

1. Go to addthis.com (see Figure 4-10).

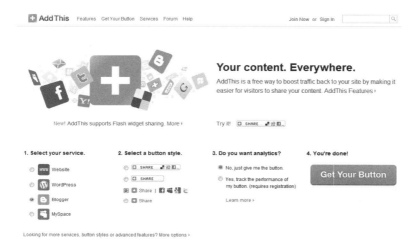

Figure 4-10. My AddThis web site

2. From Select Your Service, choose Blogger.

3. Select a button style in Step 2. They all function the same; this option is cosmetic in how you want the gadget to appear on your blog (in the Post Footer area).

4. In Step 3, leave the default to "No, just give me the button."

5. In Step 4, click Get Your Button.

6. You want it to appear under each and every post, so on the next screen click the Copy Code button under Blog Post Toolbox Instructions. Below is the code used for The Perfect Landscape example.

```
<!-- AddThis Button BEGIN -->
<div class='addthis_toolbox addthis_default_style' expr:addthis:title=
'data:post.title' expr:addthis:url='data:post.url'><a
 href='http://www.addthis.com/bookmark.php?v=250&amp;username=xa-4b9452345d8d74d7'
 class='addthis_button_compact'>Share</a>
<span class='addthis_separator'>|</span>
<a class='addthis_button_facebook'></a>
<a class='addthis_button_myspace'></a>
<a class='addthis_button_google'></a>
<a class='addthis_button_twitter'></a>
```

```
</div>
<script type="text/javascript" src="http://s7.addthis.com↵
/js/250/addthis_widget.js#username=xa-4b9452345d8d74d7"></script>
<!-- AddThis Button END -->
```

7. From within Blogger, go to the Dashboard, Design, and Edit HTML.

8. Click Expand Widgets.

9. Search for "post-footer" in the code.

10. Paste in the code so it now reads like this (paste it beneath the line for "post-footer"):

```
<div class='post-footer'>

<!-- AddThis Button BEGIN -->
<div class='addthis_toolbox addthis_default_style' expr:addthis:title=↵
'data:post.title' expr:addthis:url='data:post.url'><a ↵
href='http://www.addthis.com/bookmark.php?v=250&amp;username=↵
xa-4b9452345d8d74d7' class='addthis_button_compact'>Share</a>
<span class='addthis_separator'>|</span>
<a class='addthis_button_facebook'></a>
<a class='addthis_button_myspace'></a>
<a class='addthis_button_google'></a>
<a class='addthis_button_twitter'></a>
</div>
<script type="text/javascript" src="http://s7.addthis.com/js/250↵
/addthis_widget.js#username=xa-4b9452345d8d74d7"></script>
<!-- AddThis Button END -->
```

11. Click Save Template.

12. Click View Blog.

Integrating Social Networking

By now you have probably heard of or may be using Twitter and Facebook, two of the most popular social networking sites. So why not use them to drive traffic to your site as well? Yes, that means additional accounts to set up, manage, and post to, but it will hopefully improve your blog presence. In integrating with Facebook and Twitter, you expand your blog's visibility in that in using them people find you that may have not otherwise. For example, suppose you put your Facebook badge on your blog's sidebar and 10 of your blog readers request to be a Facebook friend. Their Facebook friends may read their wall and find out about you and become your Facebook friends as well. This type of growth and exposure can continue exponentially through Facebook networking. And while exposed on Facebook, friends may want to find out more about you and visit the web sites (blogs) you have listed on your Facebook account. Furthermore, Facebook is used to connect with friends or colleagues you haven't seen or been in contact with for some time.

Twitter is another popular networking tool in which you post small messages to your Twitter followers (personal or business). Your Twitter followers may be an entirely new set of potential customers (separate from and in addition to your Facebook friends). In the next exercise, you will add a widget using Twitter to display your last five Twitter messages (called "Tweets") in your blog's sidebar allowing your blog readers an option to follow you on Twitter or just to stay updated with what you are tweeting about.

Lastly, you will go back and edit your FeedBurner account and set it up to post automatic updates to your Twitter account. People following you on Twitter who didn't already know about your blog will then receive your blog posts. This increases your blog's exposure.

Exercise—Create a Twitter Account and Display Twitter Updates

In this exercise, you will add a gadget to your sidebar displaying the last five Tweets from your Twitter account. If you already have a Twitter account, continue to Step 7.

1. Go to `twitter.com`.

2. Click Sign Up Now.

3. Enter your full name, username, email, password, and verification text strings; accept the terms; and click Create My Account.

4. Click the Next Step: Friends button to continue.

5. Click Next Step: Others to continue.

6. Click Next Step: You're Done. Your Twitter account has now been created.

7. Go to `twitter.com/badges/typepad` and log in to Twitter.

8. Once logged in, click the View Code hyperlink and the HTML code you need will be displayed (see Figure 4-11).

9. Select and copy the code.

10. From the Dashboard, go to Design, Page Elements, and Add a Gadget.

11. Choose HTML/JavaScript.

12. Enter "Follow Me" as the title.

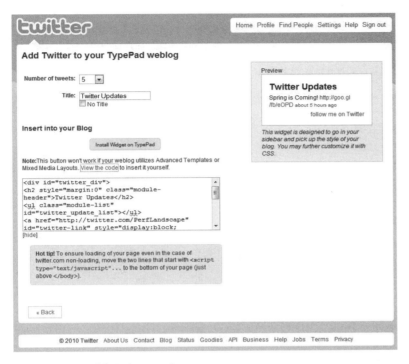

Figure 4-11. Add Twitter updates

13. Paste the code into the large text box.

14. Click Save.

15. Drag and drop where you would like the gadget to appear in your sidebar.

16. Click View Blog.

Next you will edit your FeedBurner feed to automatically post to your Twitter account. How cool is that? This will eliminate the need to post the same information in both sites. However, in addition to your blog posts, you should send other Tweets to your Twitter followers. But this isn't a book on how to use Twitter, so let's continue with modifying your FeedBurner feed.

Exercise—Adding a Twitter Account to FeedBurner Feed

In this exercise you will set up your blog's feed to post to your Twitter account:

1. Go back to feedburner.google.com. You may have to re-enter your Google password.

2. Click your existing blog feed, or if you already have it open from the earlier exercise, click the Publicize tab.

3. Click Socialize.

4. Click the Add a Twitter Account button.

5. Enter your Twitter account information (see Figure 4-12).

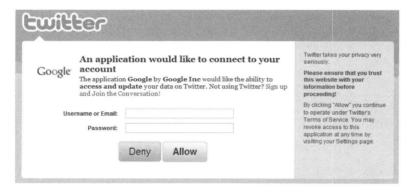

Figure 4-12. Add Twitter account to Feedburner

6. Click Allow.

7. You will see your Twitter account name as in our example for The Perfect Landscape, Twitter Account: PerfLandscape (see Figure 4-13).

8. Click the Activate button at the bottom.

9. In a few seconds, you will get the message at the top stating you have successfully updated your feed (see Figure 4-13).

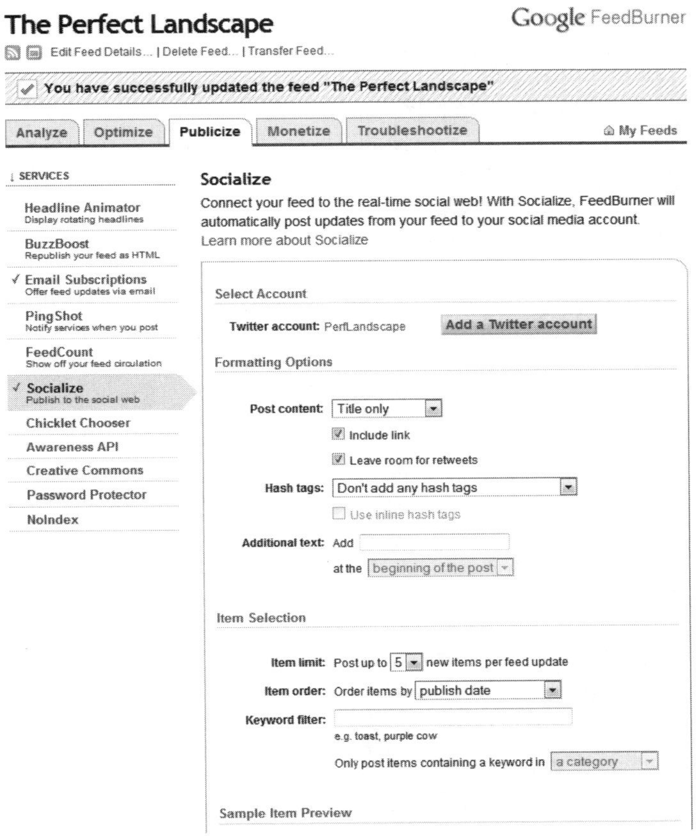

Figure 4-13. Successfully updated the feed

As a result, when you post to your blog and FeedBurner delivers the posts to your subscribers, it will automatically update your Twitter account (see Figures 4-14 and 4-15).

Figure 4-14. Spring is Coming post on Blogger

Figure 4-15. Spring is Coming Post on Twitter

Now it is time to add a Facebook Badge to your blog's sidebar. Remember, one of the reasons you add different methods of sharing your blog's content is that people use one or more different applications that people use one or more different applications, Facebook, being one of them.

Exercise—Create Facebook Account and Adding a Facebook Badge

In this exercise, you will quickly set up a Facebook account and add a Facebook Profile Badge in your blog's sidebar. If you already have a Facebook account, continue with Step 9.

1. Go to facebook.com.

2. Enter the first and last name, email, password, gender, and birthday.

3. Click the Sign Up button.

4. Enter the Security Check on the next screen.

5. Click Sign Up.

6. Enter your email password to assist in finding friends, or in this example, click Skip this Step.

7. Enter your profile information about schools and colleges you attended, or in this example, click Skip.

8. Upload your photo and click Save and Continue.

9. Click Profile and at the bottom, left click Create a Profile Badge.

10. On the right, click Edit This Badge.

11. You will see your profile image and other information.

12. Experiment by clicking different options and view the preview on the right.

13. When you're ready, click Save (see Figure 4-16) and the notice that your "Badge successfully updated."

Figure 4-16. Creating Facebook profile badge

14. Click the Blogger Logo to add to Blogger.

15. You will see the Add Page Element screen in Blogger (see Figure 4-17).

69

Figure 4-17. Add page element

16. Edit the title for the gadget if you would like. In The Perfect Landscape example, we left the default "Find Me on Facebook."

17. Click Add Widget.

18. Drag and drop where you want it in your sidebar.

19. Click Save.

20. Click on View Blog.

Visitor Tracking

Google Analytics is a free enterprise-like solution with a lot of powerful, customized reports and easy to use interface for following visitor activity. In trying to find ways to improve your blog following (and therefore increase traffic to your site) it is important to know what pages, posts, categories, or sidebar items your visitors click the most when visiting your site and how long they are staying. Those questions are probably the most important to business and blog owners, as that information is valuable in determining how to use certain areas of their blog to maximize sales for example.

In addition, you may want to install the FeedJit widget which shows demographically where people are visiting from. I think it's exciting when you learn that people in other countries are visiting your blog. With this information, in combination of what you learn from Google Analytics, you can make better marketing decisions, improve your site's design, or try to convert blog visitors into customers if you are using your blog for business purposes.

Exercise—Setting up and Adding Google Analytics

Although this book does not cover or review all the reporting and features of Google Analytics, in this exercise you will set up an account and add the necessary HTML code to your blog to best track visitor activity.

1. Visit Google Analytic's home page at google.com/analytics/.

2.   Click Access Analytics.

3.   Click Sign Up.

4.   Enter your blog's address, account name, country, and time zone (see Figure 4-18).

Google Analytics

Getting Started

Analytics: New Account Signup

General Information > Contact Information > Accept User Agreement > Add Tracking

Please enter the URL of the site you wish to track, and assign a name as it should appear in your Google Analytics reports. If you'd like to tr;

Website's URL:	http:// ▾ theperfectlandscape.blogspot.com/ (e.g. www.mywebsite.com)
Account Name:	theperfectlandscape.blogspot.cc
Time zone country or territory:	United States
Time zone:	(GMT-05:00) Eastern Time

Cancel   Continue »

Figure 4-18. Sign up for Google Analytics

5.   Click Continue.

6.   Enter your name and country and click Continue.

7.   Click the check box about accepting the Terms of Service.

8.   Click Create New Account.

9.   Leave the defaults and select and copy the HTML code (see Figure 4-19).

Figure 4-19. Tracking instructions

10. As instructed by Google in Step 2, you will be adding this before the `</body>` tag on your blog.

11. From the Dashboard, go to Design, Edit HTML.

12. Scroll down to the bottom of your page and the second to last line is `</body>`. Directly above that line, paste in the code provided for you in Step 2 (below is an example for this book and The Perfect Landscape company).

```
<script type="text/javascript">
var gaJsHost = (("https:" == document.location.protocol) ? "https://ssl."
 : "http://www.");
document.write(unescape("%3Cscript src='" + gaJsHost + "google-analytics.com/ga.js'
 type='text/javascript'%3E%3C/script%3E"));
</script>
<script type="text/javascript">
try {
var pageTracker = _gat._getTracker("UA-15101154-1");
pageTracker._trackPageview();
} catch(err) {}</script>

</body>
```

13. Click Save.

14. When you click Save and Finish in Google Analytics, you will be directed to the Analytics Settings Overview Screen (see Figure 4-20).

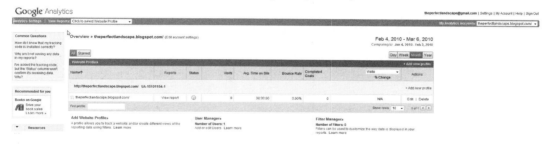

Figure 4-20. Overview of Google Analytics account

15. Although you should wait a little while before really tracking your blog (since you are still in the process of developing it), you can always come back to this page (see Figure 4-20) to view your reports.

   o Click the View Report text link.

   o You will see Site Usage categories like Visits and Page Views, as well as a pie chart of where your traffic is coming from, and more (see Figure 4-21).

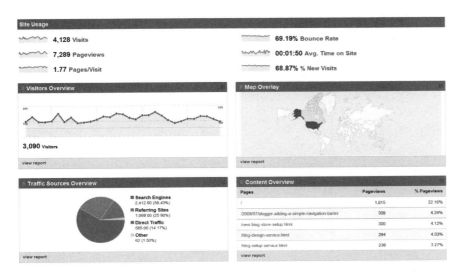

Figure 4-21. Google Analytics reports

16. If you are experiencing difficulties, visit the Common Questions area in the upper left corner.

If you need to log in to Google Analytics in the future, go to `google.com/analytics` and log in using your Google Account username and password (the same login you use for Blogger).

The next step is displaying real-time traffic information using FeedJit. In real time, this widget displays a list of visitors. No, it doesn't list their names. Instead, it will show you from where in the world they are visiting. This is not a must-have, but something fun to add to your blog and something that can still bring you valuable information about visitors to your blog. In discovering from where the majority of your visitors are coming from, you may alter promotions or revise marketing strategies.

Exercise—Adding the FeedJit Widget

Learn where your visitors are from:

1. Visit feedjit.com/ and click Get a Free Life Traffic Feed Now.

2. You can see a preview of the widget and can customize the color settings (see Figure 4-22).

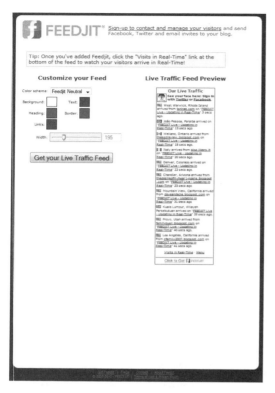

Figure 4-22. FeedJit widget

3. Click Get Your Live Traffic Feed.

4. Click Install on Blogger.

5. You will see the Add Page Element window (see Figure 4-23).

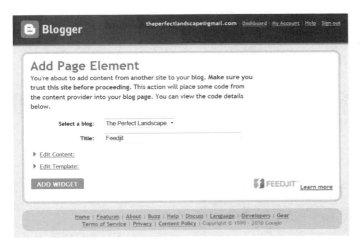

Figure 4-23. Add FeedJit Widget page element

6.   Click Add Widget.

7.   It is then added to your blog and your blog's layout will appear (where the FeedJit gadget is added and highlighted).

8.   Drag and drop the gadget where desired.

9.   Click Save.

10. Click View Blog.

Making Money

Last but not least, you will be adding the very popular Google AdSense to your blog. Content-related ads are placed on your blog in the location you choose. If someone clicks those ads, you get paid.

Although it sounds simple enough and is easy to add to your blog, you should think about it carefully before making that decision. For example, on my personal business blog (not The Perfect Landscape example), I originally had Google AdSense installed on my blog. However, I was using McAfee Site Advisor (`siteadvisor.com`) which rates search engine results and basically gives the "OK" to click a site found. It gave my site a status of Caution or Unknown. I realized it was due to Google AdSense. When I removed it, my site passed and got the green checkmark of approval. Although I know not everyone uses Internet browsing safety tools like McAfee Site Advisor, I didn't want there to be any chance of my site not being visited. Therefore I removed Google AdSense.

However, if your sole purpose of your blog is to make money and you want it to be loaded with ads, Google AdSense is free to install and will insert content-related ads to your site.

Another point to keep in mind is that depending on your blog's purpose and your type of business, you may be inserting ads linking to your competition. For example, The Perfect Landscape is a landscaping company and its blog contains tips on landscaping, gardening, and weeding. Google

AdSense will insert landscape-related ads, and in doing so may insert a link to a competing landscape business. Would you really want to do that? No!

Again, installing Google AdSense is simple, as you will see in the next exercise, but the decision to add it to your site is not.

Exercise—Adding the FeedJit Widget

Add Google AdSense to make money:

1. From the Dashboard, go to Monetize (see Figure 4-24).

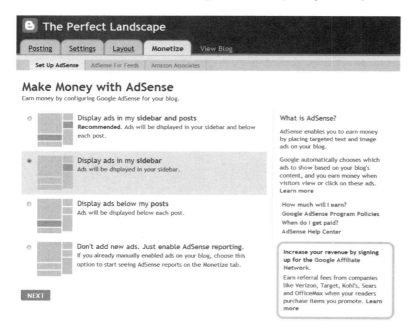

Figure 4-24. Google AdSense

2. Select a location for your ads. In our example, The Perfect Landscape, the second bullet was chosen (in the blog's sidebar).

3. Click Next.

4. Click Create a New AdSense Account.

5. Enter all information including your name, address, country, etc. (see Figure 4-25)

6. Click Submit Information.

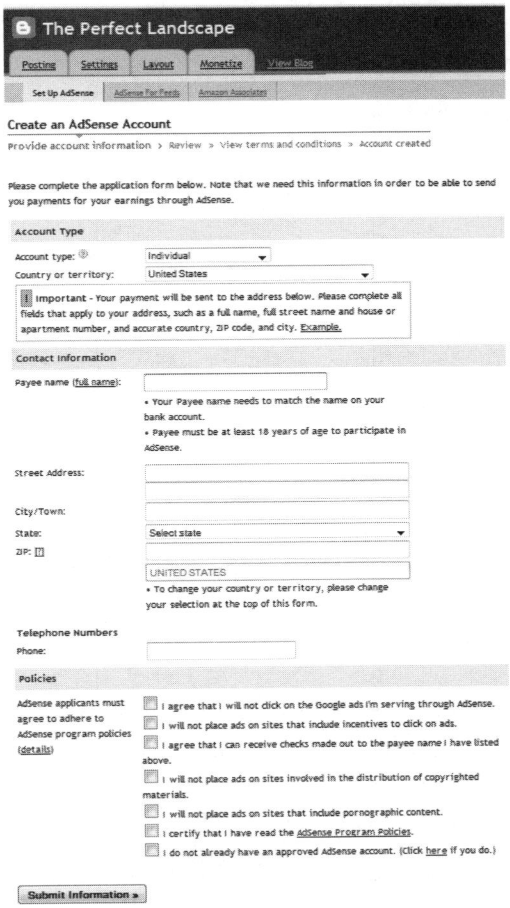

B The Perfect Landscape

Posting   Settings   Layout   Monetize   View Blog

Set Up AdSense   AdSense For Feeds   Amazon Associates

Create an AdSense Account

Provide account information > Review > View terms and conditions > Account created

Please complete the application form below. Note that we need this information in order to be able to send you payments for your earnings through AdSense.

Account Type

Account type: ⑦   Individual
Country or territory: United States

❗ Important - Your payment will be sent to the address below. Please complete all fields that apply to your address, such as a full name, full street name and house or apartment number, and accurate country, ZIP code, and city. Example.

Contact Information

Payee name (full name):

• Your Payee name needs to match the name on your bank account.
• Payee must be at least 18 years of age to participate in AdSense.

Street Address:

City/Town:

State: Select state

ZIP: ⑦

UNITED STATES

• To change your country or territory, please change your selection at the top of this form.

Telephone Numbers

Phone:

Policies

AdSense applicants must agree to adhere to AdSense program policies (details)

☐ I agree that I will not click on the Google ads I'm serving through AdSense.
☐ I will not place ads on sites that include incentives to click on ads.
☐ I agree that I can receive checks made out to the payee name I have listed above.
☐ I will not place ads on sites involved in the distribution of copyrighted materials.
☐ I will not place ads on sites that include pornographic content.
☐ I certify that I have read the AdSense Program Policies.
☐ I do not already have an approved AdSense account. (Click here if you do.)

Submit Information »

Figure 4-25. Create an AdSense account

7. On the next screen, verify that the information is correct.

8. Click Create Account.

9. Review the Terms and Conditions.

10. Check the box at the bottom about accepting the terms.

11. Click the I Accept button.

12. On the next screen, your AdSense account is enabled on your blog (see Figure 4-26), however they will not appear on your blog for another 48 hours.

13. Click Edit Layout to move it around in your sidebar.

14. Click Save.

The Perfect Landscape

Posting | Settings | Layout | **Monetize** | View Blog

AdSense Overview | AdSense For Feeds | Amazon Associates

AdSense is enabled for your blog!

Your ads are currently serving with publisher ID *ca-pub-9076056021948053*.

Please wait up to 48 hours for your new account to be reviewed before ads are displayed on your blog. In the meantime, your blog will display public service announcements in place of ads. **Learn more.**

To modify the location or display of your ads, go to the **Layout > Page Elements** tab. From there, you can edit existing AdSense gadgets, add additional AdSense gadgets through the gadget directory, or modify the display of ads in your posts. For specific instructions, please view our **help article.**

View Blog (in a new window) | **Edit Layout**

AdSense Reports | Switch AdSense Account | Customize/Add Ads | Remove Ads | Help

Figure 4-26. AdSense is enabled

Summary

Wow! You learned a lot today! It is very important to learn new ways of driving traffic to your blog, keeping existing readers, learning about visitor activity, and integrating with Twitter and Facebook (as well as other social networking sites through the AddThis gadget).

In addition to all the new gadgets added to your blog, you also learned how to use the traditional meta tags (keywords and description) to help rank your site and how to create an effective post. As stressed in earlier chapters, blogging is all about posting. It is just as important to create a well-written post as it is to post often.

Another source of improving your blog's visibility is using a Blogroll or simply asking others to link to your site. The more sites that contain a link back to your blog, the more likely you are to reach new visitors and potential customers. And in following that concept, you turned on Backlinks as another way of showing and tracking other blogs linking to yours.

Google Analytics is a powerful tool allowing you to review visitor activity. Someone could write a book on that alone! Seriously, it is important to learn where your visitors click, how long they stay on your blog, what time or day of the week they visit, and more. This information can prove to be very helpful in making business decisions or adjusting a current business plan.

Lastly, you learned how to quickly set up AdSense, which places relevant ads based on your blog's content. In the next chapter, you will learn how to use a custom domain name with your blog instead of the default Blogger address (blogspot address).

CHAPTER 5

Setting Up a Custom Domain

Many Blogger users, after setting up their blog, do not like that the word "BlogSpot" is in their Internet address (such as theperfectlandscape.blogspot.com or www.theperfectlandscape.com). Instead, they want it to read theperfectlandscape.com. This is possible to do in Blogger. If you don't already have a domain name registered, such as theperfectlandscape.com, you may quickly and easily purchase one within Blogger using Google Apps. If you purchase or have already purchased a domain name from another domain registrant like GoDaddy or Network Solutions, it can be mapped to your Blogger blog.

Don't worry; these terms will be explained in brief and detailed, step-by-step instructions provided on how to set up a custom domain to work with Blogger.

Terminology

You do not have to be a technically savvy person to be able to set up your domain name, but it may help to know and understand a few of the terms used in the following exercises.

- Domain name: This is the name you would like for your blog. In my example, I used the-perfect-landscape.com.

- Domain: This refers to the last section of your domain name. In The Perfect Landscape example, the ".com" domain suffix was desired and is the most commonly used. The ".net" domain suffix is likely second in popularity and derived from "Internet." The ".org," ".gov," and ".edu" suffixes are also popular domains, where ".org" is commonly used for non-profit organizations; ".gov" for government offices; and ".edu" for educational facilities, universities, or programs.

- Domain registrars: These are companies (like Go Daddy, Network Solutions, Yahoo! Small Business, 1 & 1, and many others) that host or manage domain names for you for an annual fee. Basically, you are buying the domain name from them to use for your blog.

To apply these terms to our example, you will be purchasing a custom domain from Google Apps, GoDaddy, or another domain registrar for an annual fee. In The Perfect Landscape example, the .com domain was used and the domain name the-perfect-landscape.com was purchased and set up to be used with The Perfect Landscape Blogger blog.

Custom Domain

You can map or associate your domain name (custom domain) to your Blogger blog address. You can do this in one of two ways depending on whether you have already purchased your domain through a domain registrar, like GoDaddy, or if you will be purchasing a domain name now (as in the exercise below) through Google Apps.

Setting Up a New Domain

In the following exercise, you will purchase and publish your blog to a custom domain through Google Apps. When choosing a domain name, it is good practice to have it be the same name as your blog's title or blog address if the domain name is available.

Exercise—Purchase and Use a Custom Domain

In this exercise, you will purchase and set up a custom domain to be used with your Blogger blog:

1. From the Dashboard, click Settings.

2. Click Publishing and you will see controls (see Figure 5-1).

Figure 5-1. Publishing on Blogspot.com

3. Click on text link Custom Domain. You'll see the screen for buying your own domain (see Figure 5-2).

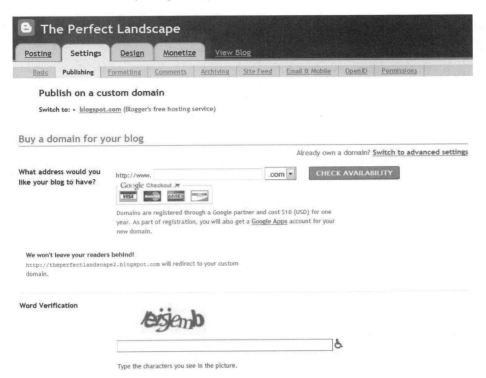

Figure 5-2. Publish on a custom domain

4. In the "What address would you like your blog to have?" text box, type the domain name you would like to register. In our example, the-perfect-landscape.com was used.

5. Click Check Availability. If the domain name is not available or taken, other suggestions will be presented. Choose one and click Continue.

6. When you find an available domain name, you will see a new screen (see Figure 5-3).

Choose a domain name (step 1 of 3)

✓ **the-perfect-landscape.com is available**

- One year domain registration for **$10**
- Private domain registration to protect against spam at no extra cost
- Full DNS control and domain management
- Automatically configured to work with Google services
- Email, calendar, instant messaging, web pages and more also at no extra charge

Need more details? Learn more

[Continue to registration]   powered by GoDaddy.com Learn more

Figure 5-3. Welcome to Google Apps, domain available

7. Click Continue to Registration (note that the registration is powered by GoDaddy.com).

8. Enter your contact information (see Figure 5-4).

Figure 5-4. *Enter domain registration information*

9. Be sure to check off that you have read the GoDaddy Universal Terms of Service.

10. Check off if you want your account to automatically renew each year.

11. Read the Google Terms of Service.

12. Click I Agree. Proceed to Google Checkout.

13. Enter your credit card information (see Figure 5-5).

Figure 5-5. Google Checkout, add a credit card

14. Click Agree and Continue.

15. You'll be asked to re-enter your login information for your Google Account (see Figure 5-6).

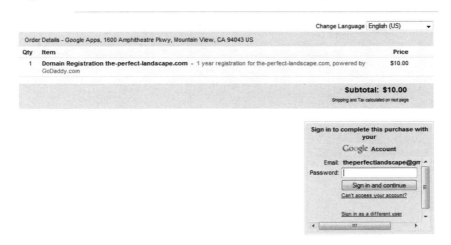

Figure 5-6. Sign in to your Google account

16. Click Sign In and Continue.

17. Click Pay Your Order Now ($10).

18. You will receive a "You're Done!" message.

19. Click Return to Google Apps to manage your domain in the next exercise of mapping your domain to your blog.

20. You are brought back to your blog, Settings, and the Publishing tab where you will see a confirmation that your domain purchase is complete (see Figure 5-7).

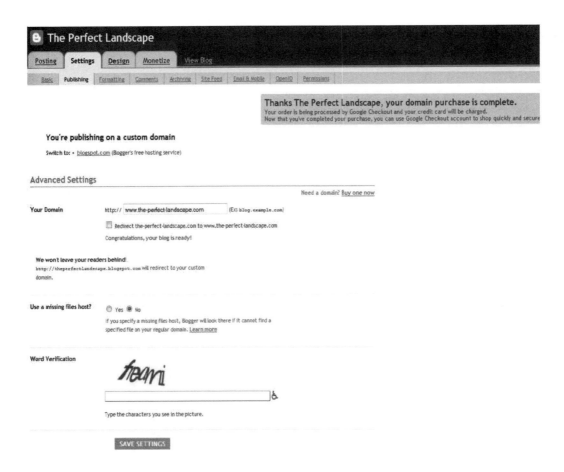

Figure 5-7. Domain purchase is complete

21. Under Your Domain (see the-perfect-landscape.com in Figure 5-7, click the check box that will redirect your non-"www" address to your domain name with the "www" in its name. For example "Redirect the-perfect-landscape.com to www.the-perfect-landscape.com."

22. Enter the Word Verification.

23. Click Save Settings.

24. Although you just purchased and set up the custom domain, it is not quite ready yet. A Blogger window will appear with the message "Your blog is in transition." But within the next few days, your domain will activate.

You're now done. That's all you needed to do to set up your personal or business domain. In our example for The Perfect Landscape, visitors may visit the blog using any of the following addresses:

- `the-perfect-landscape.com`
- `www.the-perfect-landscape.com`
- `theperfectlandscape.blogspot.com`

Using an Existing Domain

Many people purchase a domain name before owning or operating a blog or web site to reserve the name they want while it is available. The following exercise assumes that you have previously purchased a domain from another registrar (like GoDaddy or Network Solutions) and that you would like to use it with your Blogger blog.

Exercise—Using an Existing Domain Name with Blogger

This is a two-step process: A CNAME (Canonical Name) record needs to be added in your domain manager, and you need to set up your custom domain in Blogger.

1. Go to the web site where you registered your domain. You will need to add a CNAME record under DNS (Domain Name System) settings. In GoDaddy, this is through the Domain Manager and under the Total DNS Control and MX Records area. In other companies, it may be called Zone File Manager, Domain Manager, or DNS Settings.

2. View Blogger help (`google.com/support/blogger/bin/answer.py?hl=en&answer=58317`) for step-by-step instructions on how to add a CNAME record for a few popular domain registrars, such as GoDaddy and Yahoo! Small Business.

3. In general, you will edit or add a CNAME record for "www".

4. Have it Point To: ghs.google.com.

5. Save changes.

6. Go to Blogger.

7. From the Dashboard, go to Settings and then Publishing.

8. Click Custom Domain.

9. Under the "Buying a domain for your blog" section (see Figure 5-2), to the right under "Already have a domain?", click Switch to Advanced Settings.

10. For Domain Name, enter your domain using the "www." but without the "http://" as in `www.the-perfect-landscape.com`.

11. Enter the Word Verification.

12. Save Settings.

13. View Blog to see if your blog comes up. It is normally an immediate update.

14. From the Publishing tab, click the check box for redirecting the "non-www" address to the URL with the "www" in it.

15. Enter the Word Verification.

16. Save Settings again.

You're done! That's all you needed to do to connect your personal or business domain to your Blogger blog. In our example for The Perfect Landscape, visitors may visit that blog with any of the following addresses:

- `theperfectlandscape.com`

- `www.the-perfect-landscape.com`

- `the-perfect-landscape.blogspot.com`

Summary

Although it is not required to have a custom domain used with your Blogger blog, many users want to set one up at some point after the blog is created. There are many domain registrar companies in which you can purchase a domain name, however one of the most convenient is purchasing one from within Blogger through Google Apps. The steps for buying and setting up a custom domain within Blogger are detailed in the first exercise. When the set up is complete, your blog readers can visit your blog using the original BlogSpot address, or by using the new domain name with or without the leading "www" in the Internet address. In the Chapter 6, you will learn about Blogger's image storage and management, and how and where Blogger stores your blog's images. These concepts need to be addressed and understood before advancing through the remainder of this book.

■■■

Working with Images

I'm sure you have created a few of your own posts and inserted a few images either as part of your posts or in your blog's sidebar. Where are they being stored? What happens when you delete an image? How many images can you post, or is there a storage size limitation? These questions and more will be addressed in this chapter.

You will be using Google's Picasa Web Albums and Google Sites to store and use images for your blog, both of which are free services. In this chapter, you will view where they are stored and how to manage them, and also create additional photo albums. In addition, you may want to use images on your blog that you do not want stored in an album or taking up your Blogger image storage space. In this case, you will learn how to upload images to Google Sites and how to use and reference those online images.

Using Picasa Web Albums

In Chapter 2, you learned how to insert images into your posts and how to upload your profile image. Although Blogger does not currently have a file manager, your images are being stored online. All images manually inserted into your blog via posts, the Picture gadget, or profile image are being stored in Picasa Web Albums.

Picasa Web Albums is a tool Blogger uses to store images and allows you to share photos. Albums related to your blog(s) are denoted with the Blogger logo. In addition, you can create your own albums that store images not on your blog, Later, you can create a link to them from your blog or embed HTML code into your blog.

There are a few things to remember when working with Picasa Web Albums and inserting and deleting Blogger images. Even if you delete a picture from your blog (for example a post), it is not automatically deleted from the album. Also, if you insert the same image more than once, it is uploaded and stored to your blog's Picasa Web Album that many times as well. For example, if you've inserted the same image three times, it then appears in your album three times. This is of concern for two reasons. First, if you decide to create a slideshow for the album, the same picture would appear multiple times. Second, and more importantly, is your Blogger blog has a default maximum storage limit of 1024MB. This is considered a significant amount of space, but you still want to keep in mind that there is a limit. Furthermore, do not delete items from your blog's Picasa Web Album without first deleting them from your blog. If you do, you will see the empty image place holder (the red "x" where an image used to be).

■ **Note** By default, your Blogger albums are not made public, however you may change the setting to make them public or add them to Google's image search (Blogger or Picasa Web Albums).

Exercise—Viewing Blogger Images

In this exercise, you will log in to Picasa Web Albums and view the default album(s) used by your Blogger blog(s):

1. From the Dashboard, under Other Stuff, Picasa Web Albums is listed under Tools and Resources.

2. Click Picasa Web Albums or go to picasawebalbum.google.com.

3. Log in using your Blogger password if you are prompted for it.

4. Click Sign in.

5. You will see one or two albums; one with the name of your blog (in our example, "The Perfect Landscape"), and the other that says "Blogger Pictures" (see Figure 6-1).

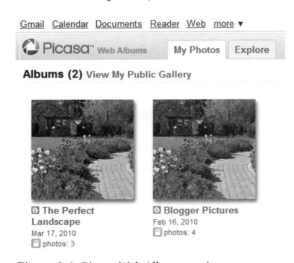

Figure 6-1. Picasa Web Albums main screen

6. In this example, the Blogger Pictures album has four pictures, all the same. It inserted them when the profile image for The Perfect Landscape was added. In your Blogger Pictures album, you should see your profile image if you uploaded one in Chapter 2.

7. Click Blogger Pictures to view what is in your album.

8. To go back to the main screen where it lists all your albums (for now there should be two at most since we haven't created a new one yet), click My Photos.

9. You should see an album with the Blogger logo next to the name of your blog, such as The Perfect Landscape (see Figure 6-1).

10. To open it, click the album. In the album, you should see all images that have been inserted into your blog either in posts, in the banner, on the sidebar using the Picture Gadget, etc.

11. In our example of The Perfect Landscape, there is the picture of the same image used in the first post, which also happens to be the profile image, as well as two that were used for the banner (see Figure 6-2).

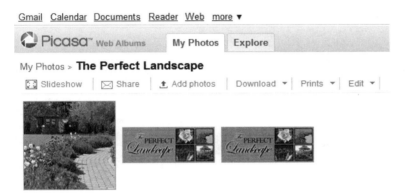

Figure 6-2. The Perfect Landscape album

12. The two banner pictures illustrate the way in which Blogger stores images, meaning one version of the banner was added and removed and another version that was resized and uploaded. Blogger never removed the old image from the Picasa Web Album; therefore there are two appearing in the album.

Again, keep in mind that deleting or removing an image from your blog does not mean it is automatically removed from the corresponding Blogger Picasa Web albums. You must go to Picasa Web Albums and delete the images there.

While using Picasa Web Albums and inserting, deleting, and managing images, notice that when you are at the main screen (My Photos) near the bottom, and center, it displays and keeps track of your storage space—how much you have used (see Figure 6-3). If you ever run out of space, you can upgrade (buy space) at reasonable rates (such as 20 MB (megabytes) for $5 a year).

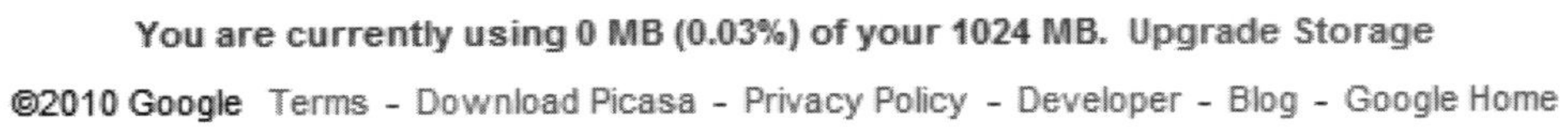

You are currently using 0 MB (0.03%) of your 1024 MB. Upgrade Storage

©2010 Google Terms – Download Picasa – Privacy Policy – Developer – Blog – Google Home

Figure 6-3. *Picasa Web album storage space monitoring*

■ **Note** In addition to using the online version of Picasa Web Albums to manage and store blog images, you can also download Picasa's photo editing and sharing software. Visit picasa.google.com/features.html to learn more. It's free.

In addition to having your blog images uploaded to your blog's Picasa Web album, you can manually insert images into the album as well. One reason for doing this is if you wanted to create a slideshow from the album to then place on your blog's sidebar.

Exercise—Adding Images and Creating Slideshows

In this exercise, you will open an existing album and insert more images and create a slideshow to add to your blog:

1. While at the main screen where you can view all your albums, click the album with your blog's name. In our example, it would be "The Perfect Landscape" album.

2. Click Add Photos.

3. Using this online method for uploading pictures, you can upload five at a time (see Figure 6-4).

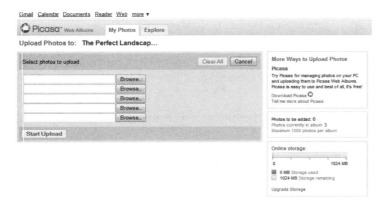

Figure 6-4. *Uploading images*

4. Click the Browse button to upload your first image.

5. Locate the file on your computer. Select it and click Open.

6. If you have more files to upload, continue clicking the Browse button and locating the files.

7. When you have finished selecting the files to add, click Start Upload.

8. When the upload is complete, the pictures are added to the album and displayed (see Figure 6-5).

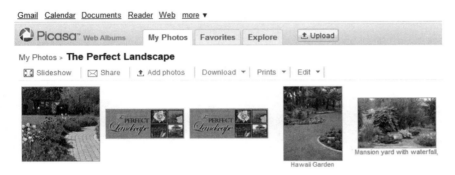

Figure 6-5. Images added

9. Next, you'll create a slideshow to add to your blog's sidebar.

10. While the album is still open, click Link to This Album on the right sidebar (see Figure 6-6).

11. Select Embed Slideshow and select Small for the size so it will fit in your sidebar (see Figure 6-7).

12. Select and copy the HTML code provided. Click Done.

13. Go back to Blogger.

14. From the Dashboard, click Design, and go to Page Elements.

15. Click Add a Gadget (in the sidebar area) and choose HTML/JavaScript.

16. Paste in the code you just copied from Picasa Web Album into the Content area. Enter "Gallery" for the title (see Figure 6-8).

Figure 6-6. Link to this album

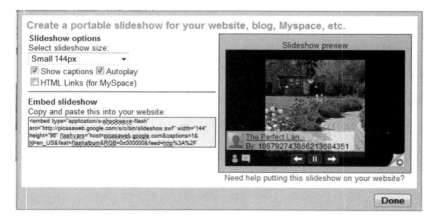

Figure 6-7. Create slideshow to embed

Figure 6-8. Configure HTML/JavaScript gadget

17. Click Save.

18. It is added to the top of your sidebar.

19. Drag and drop the gadget to a desired location in the sidebar.

20. Save changes by clicking Save.

21. Click View Blog to view the newly added slideshow (see Figure 6-9).

Figure 6-9. Embedded slideshow

In the previous example, you added new pictures to an existing album. There may be times when you want to create a new album separate from your blog pictures, including one for family pictures or featured products for your business. In this next exercise, a new album for The Perfect Landscape will be added and various pictures of projects will be stored before and after completion.

Exercise—Creating a New Album

In this exercise, you will upload pictures to a new album and create a link to it that can be used in a post:

1. While in Picasa Web albums, click the Upload button.

2. You can select an existing album to add pictures to, however in this example click the Create a New Album hyperlink.

3. Give the album a name in the title field and enter a description if you would like (see Figure 6-10).

4. Where it says "Share," the default setting is "Public" meaning it is accessible to everyone. You can set it to "Unlisted" if you want to keep it private (however, in that case you would not create a link to it from your blog).

5. Click Continue.

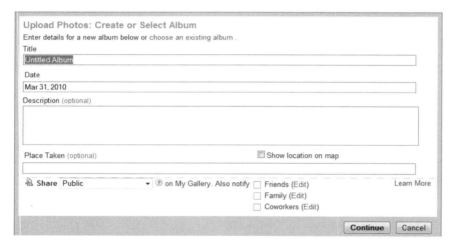

Figure 6-10. Creating a new album

6. Upload pictures as you did in the previous exercise.

7. When finished selecting pictures, click Upload.

8. You could then create a slideshow as you previously had done or create a link to the album to later use in a post.

9. Click Link to This Album. Select and copy the URL in Paste link in email or IM

10. Go back to Blogger and create a new post. In that post, enter text such as "Click here to . . ."

11. Select "Click here" and click the Link button from the toolbar and paste in the URL.

12. Continue your post and publish when finished.

13. View Blog to test your new link.

You can create as many albums as you like as long as you don't exceed the maximum storage limit (1024 MB).

Next, you may wish to delete an image. Click the desired image. From the Edit Menu, choose "Delete this photo" and click "OK" to confirm the deletion.

Although there is still more you can do with Picasa Web Albums, such as printing and ordering photos, we'll only discuss in this chapter how to set your Blogger albums to public. This is done under Edit Menu and choosing Album Properties. You can then set the share value to "Public" as shown in the previous exercise. If you would like more information and help with Picasa Web Albums, visit `picasa.google.com/support/?hl=en_US`.

Google Sites

Although Google Sites is a free tool to help you build a traditional web site, you will be using it to store large pictures. From personal experience, I had trouble with Picasa Web Albums and services like Photobucket and Flickr when trying to load a large image, such as one used for a custom blog background (for example 1920 px by 1200 px). A friend of mine, Michelle Laycock of Laycock Designs, recommended Google Sites because it is a service she uses for her clients. In Chapter 7, we will review how to install the custom background and other custom graphics for your blog that will be uploaded to Google Sites. In the next exercise, we'll upload the background image.

Exercise—Uploading Image to Google Sites

It is easier to manage all custom graphics for your site in one place and since larger images may be needed, you will be using Google Sites:

1. Since you are logged into Blogger (owned by Google), go to `sites.google.com` and re-enter your password if necessary.

2. Click Create Site. (See Figure 6-11).

Figure 6-11. Creating a Google Site

3. Give your site a name such as the name of your blog (no spaces). If that name is not available, try variations or use their suggestions until you find one.

4. Since we are not using this site as an actual web site and only for storage, you do not need to choose a template or theme, so keep the defaults.

5. Enter the code (characters) shown.

6. Click Create Site.

7. Don't worry about creating an actual site. We are just uploading images. From the More Actions dropdown box in the upper right corner of your screen, click Manage Site (see Figure 6-12).

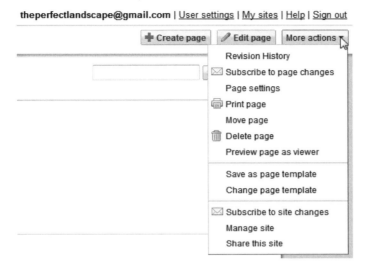

Figure 6-12. More Actions menu

8. From the left sidebar, click Attachments (see Figure 6-13).

Figure 6-13. Attachments

9. Click the Upload button.

10. Locate a file on your computer by clicking Browse, such as a background image you want to use for your blog.

11. Click Open once you have selected a file.

12. Click Upload.

13. Notice the file is now uploaded (see Figure 6-14) and listed in the Attachments section.

Figure 6-14. Uploaded attachment

14. In Chapter 7, when you need to install the background and learn other advanced layout techniques, you will click View to get the image's URL.

15. For now, click View just to preview the image (although we will not do anything further at this point).

Figure 6-15. Custom background for The Perfect Landscape

16. Close the image preview.

17. You can close Google Sites if you would like, but do not click Sign Out as that will log you out of Blogger.

If there are other custom graphics you have designed for your blog, upload them here as you will use them in the next chapter.

Summary

Now you know that when you post images to your blog, add a banner, upload your profile image, or insert pictures in your sidebar (with the Picture gadget), those images are stored by Blogger in a Picasa Web Album. You can delete or add images from those albums and create additional albums.

In this chapter, we learned how to create a slideshow from an album and how to insert it into your blog's sidebar (by adding a HTML/JavaScript gadget).

The most important thing I want you to remember from this chapter is that when you delete images from your blog, they are not automatically deleted from the corresponding Picasa Web Album, and they are still taking up storage space until you manually delete them. On the same note, you do not want to delete images from your Blogger Picasa Web albums (those labeled with your blog's name or Blogger Pictures) before deleting them from your blog. If you do this, the images will not be available and your blog readers will see the empty image placeholder.

Lastly, we reviewed how to upload images to Google Sites, including a custom background for your blog. In the following chapter, you will learn how to install a background and other graphics to improve the overall look of your blog.

■■■

CHAPTER 7

Advanced Design and Layout

In the last chapter, you finished uploading a custom background image to Google Sites. In this chapter, you will learn how to install it and modify your Blogger template using CSS and HTML. You do not have to be an HTML expert to make these changes, but if you are interested in learning more, I highly recommend visiting w3schools.com.

This chapter is heavily concentrated on installing or adding graphics to your blog to give it an edge and a completely customized look. This can be done by installing a horizontal image to separate your posts (called a post separator); adding an image background for your sidebar titles; and installing pre-made backgrounds, banners, or templates from popular sites. This involves modifying the HTML and CSS code in your Blogger template, as well as uploading graphics to Google Sites or another image-sharing site you may be using, and finally referencing them in your code.

This chapter is packed with information and changes to code in your Blogger template. Make sure you've had your coffee first!

Install Blogger Templates

Yes, Blogger has a beautiful Template Designer; however, you may not have found a template you envisioned for your business or one that suited your personality. There are plenty of sites offering free templates, backgrounds, banners, and more. In this part of the chapter, we'll quickly review how to install graphics from online sources I have personally used including The Cutest Blog on the Block, eBlog Templates, and Blogger Templates Free.

A great advantage to using templates is that you do not have to create your own graphics or spend hours manually customizing and experimenting with code.

■ **Note:** Before making any changes to your current blog layout, it is always a good idea to create a backup. From the Dashboard, go to Design, then Edit HTML, and click on Download Full Template which stores an XML file to your computer. If you ever need to restore the template, click Browse to find the XML file, then click Upload.

The Cutest Blog on the Block

This is a very popular, cute, and fun site that has a lot of free options for Blogger, Twitter, and MySpace including free backgrounds. What's even better than having so many to choose from (two- and three-column layouts) is that they are so easy to install.

Exercise—Installing a Free Background from The Cutest Blog on the Block

To use backgrounds from The Cutest Blog on the Block, change your Blogger template to Minima and copy and paste the site's code into a new HTML/JavaScript gadget.

1. With Blogger, go to Design and Edit HTML.

2. Scroll to the bottom under Old Templates, and click on Select Layout Template.

3. Choose Minima (first template).

4. Click Save Template.

5. Go to TheCutestBlogontheBlock.com to get started.

6. Click Backgrounds from the menu, then choose Blogger.

7. Scroll down to view the free backgrounds on the opening page. They are categorized on the right-hand side, or you can use the Keyword Search (see Figure 7-1).

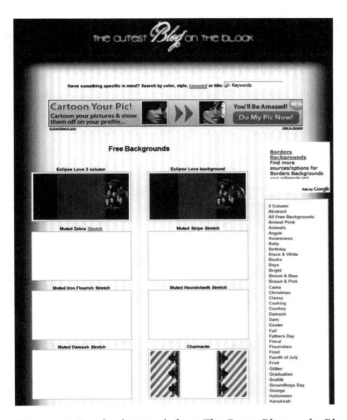

Figure 7-1. Free backgrounds from The Cutest Blog on the Block

8. Find one you like and click it. In The Perfect Landscape example, Subtle Stripes was selected

9. Go to Copy and Paste This Code box. Select all the code and Copy. Here is the code used for Subtle Stripes (see Figure 7-2).

```
<script>document.write(unescape("%3Cstyle%20type%3D%22text/css%22%3E%0Abody%20%7B
  background-image %3A%20url%28%22http%3A//i342.photobucket.com/albums/o401/
Thecutestblogontheblock/backgroundensignbookscopy-1.jpg %22%29%3B
%20background-position%3A%20center%3B%20background-repeat%3A%20no-repeat%3B%20
  background-attachment %3A%20fixed%3B%20%7D%0A%3C/style%3E%0A%3Cdiv
%20id%3D%22tag%22%20 style%3D%22position%3Aabsolute %3B%20left%3A0px%3B%20top
%3A30px%3B%20z-index%3A50%3B%20 width%3A150px%3B%20height%3A45px%3B%22
%3E%0A%3Ca%20href%3D%22 http%3A//www.thecutestblogontheblock.com
%22%20target%3D%22_blank%22%3E%0A%3Cimg%20src %3D%22http%3A
//www.thecutestblogontheblock.com/images/tag.png%22%20border%3D%220%22/
%3E%0A%3C/a%3E%3C/div%3E%20"));</script>
```

10. Go back to your Blogger blog and click Page Elements.

11. Go to the Footer area and click Add a Gadget.

12. In Title enter <!--background--> (it will not appear on your blog), and paste the code into the Content box.

13. Click Save.

14. View your blog (see Figure 7-2).

15. To remove the background and bring your blog back to the original layout, remove the gadget you just added.

16. Click Save and view blog.

Figure 7-2. The Cutest Blog on the Block free background installed

Because it is easy to install new backgrounds, try experimenting with a few until you find one you like. If you find one you like but do not like that the middle is not white, you can add this code to the outer wrapper area: `background: #FFFFFF`. You will learn how to modify CSS code like this later in this chapter in the "Convert to a Three-Column Format" exercise.

Have fun experimenting with The Cutest Blog on the Block as the site has many designs and many of the backgrounds have available matching banners.

eBlog Templates

If you are looking for professional, business-quality templates, eBlog Templates is the site you must visit! It is loaded with many designs. I am sure you will find one that suits your business or personal style.

Templates include graphics and color scheme (see Figure 7-3 which has the Peaceful Rush template installed). Notice the banner image, background image, and that the color for the post title and links are already set to match the banner. Once you have installed a template, you may later customize it. These templates are easy to install and can quickly provide your blog with a professional look.

Exercise—Using an eBlog Template

In this exercise you will install an eBlog Template.

1. Go to eBlogTemplates.com and from the menu bar choose Blogger and All Blogger Templates.

2. Scroll through the templates until you find one you like. You can click the Live Demo hyperlink in the right sidebar to preview a larger, real size view of the template.

3. I chose Peaceful Rush for this exercise and for The Perfect Landscape blog. Click Download Now and you will be prompted to save or open a zip (compressed) file. Many computers come with software to open zip files, however if you need one, go to WinZip.com.

4. Save the file to your computer. Open the downloaded file (peaceful-rush.zip) and extract (save) the peaceful-rush.xml file to your computer.

5. Go to Edit HML. Click Download Full Template to save a backup of your current layout and blog design.

6. Click Browse and select the peaceful-rush.xml file you just saved.

7. Click Upload.

8. Blogger will inform you that certain widgets don't exist in this template and will ask what you want to do with them. Choose Keep Widgets.

9. Go to Page Elements and rearrange the sidebar items again by dragging and dropping them where you would like. Click Save when you have completed your changes.

10. Click View Blog to view the new design.

Figure 7-3. The Perfect Landscape with the Peaceful Rush Template installed

Blogger Templates Free

Like eBlog Templates, Blogger Templates Free also includes a plentiful selection of high-quality templates. I like how they are categorized on the right sidebar so you can quickly look at templates of interest.

These template packages include the graphics used in the templates, as well as the coordinating color scheme embedded in the XML file. You many continue customizing the template.

Exercise—Installing a Blogger Templates Free Template

In this exercise, you will install a custom template from Blogger Templates Free.

1. Go to bloggertemplatesfree.com.

2. On the right, the templates are categorized to help find the designs you are looking for.

3. In this exercise, the Outono design will be used (found under the Elegant category).

4. When you click it (Outono), you may also click Live Demo to view an enlarged, live version.

5. Click Download and you will be prompted to save or open a zip (compressed) file.

6. Save the file to your computer. Open the downloaded file (Outono.zip).

7. Open the Outono folder found inside, and another Outono folder will be found. Open the folders until you find the outono.xml file.

8. Choose to extract (save) the file to your computer. There is a ReadMe.txt file and an Images folder. The images are hosted on the site's servers so you do not need them, although they are still provided. You may want to use them for other projects or newsletters. The main point is you want the XML file!

9. Switch to Blogger, go to Edit HTML, and click Download Full Template to save a backup of your current layout and blog design.

10. Click Browse and select the outono.xml file you just saved.

11. Click Upload.

12. Blogger will inform you that certain widgets don't exist in the template and will ask what you want to do with them. Choose Keep Widgets.

13. View your blog. If you have installed a custom banner and it overlays the new template header area, go back to Page Elements and remove the image.

    a. Click Edit on the Header element and where you see a preview of the custom banner image, click the Remove Image link (see Figure 7-4).

    b. Click Save.

14. Click View Blog to view your new blog design (see Figure 7-5).

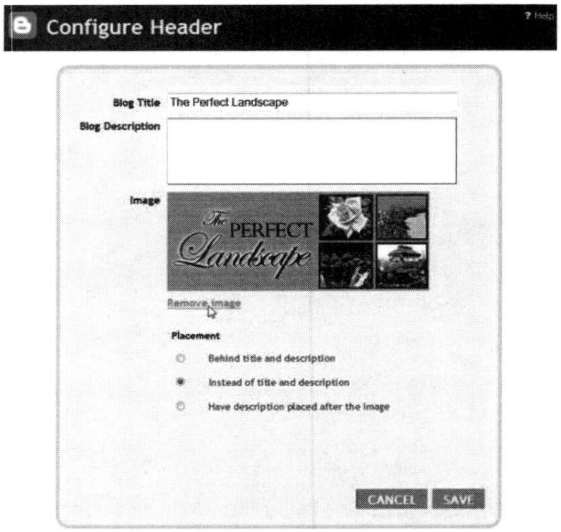

Figure 7-4. Remove image

Figure 7-5. The Perfect Landscape with the Outono template installed

Now that you have tested a few templates, we're going to pick it up a notch and manually update your blog's design using CSS and HTML code including images stored to Google Sites.

Install a Background

In the last exercise of Chapter 6, you uploaded a custom background to Google Sites (see Figure 6-15). We will now modify your blog's layout in order to use it. First, open Google Sites (sites.google.com).

Currently your blog may look something like The Perfect Landscapes' (see Figure 7-5) using one of the Blogger Free Templates.

In the next exercise, you will convert your blog back to the Minima template (see Figure 7-6), make minor adjustments to CSS code, and reference the recently uploaded Google Sites image (background) to change the look of your blog (see Figure 7-7).

Exercise—Install a Custom Background

There are a few things we need to do. (See Figure 7-8 for an example of a custom background.)

- Change to the Minima Blogger template (see Figure 7-6).

- Log in to Google Sites and get the URL address for the recently uploaded image (to be used as your blog's background).

- Modify the CSS code in order to install the background and use it in your blog layout.

Let's get started:

1. If you are not already logged in, log in to your Blogger account.

2. From the Dashboard, go to Design.

3. Go to Edit HTML, scroll to the bottom under Old Templates, click on Select Layout Template, then choose Minima. You had done this earlier in this chapter when installing a template from The Cutest Blog on the Block.

Figure 7-6. Minima Template selected

4. Click Save Template.

5. Get the image's URL from Google Sites by going <u>to</u> sites.google.com. You may have to re-enter your password to sign in.

6. Click your site.

7. From under More Actions in the upper-right corner, click Manage Site.

8. Click Attachments and you will see the custom background we previously uploaded in Chapter 6.

9. Right-click View and choose Copy Link Location or Copy Shortcut depending on which Internet browser you are using (see Figure 7-7).

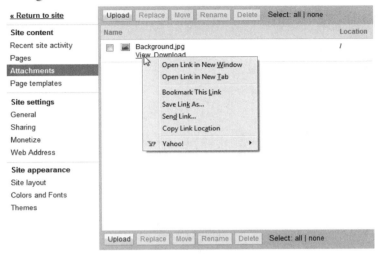

Figure 7-7. Copy link location from Google Sites

10. Go back to Blogger and click Edit HTML.

11. You will be modifying this line of code:

```
body {
background:$bgcolor;
```

12. To read like this instead, comments are added between the /* and */.

```
body {
 background: url(http://sites.google.com/site/theperfectlandscape/Background.jpg);
 /* setting the body's background (which is the main blog's page background) to the⏎
 image from Google Sites */
 background-position: top center;  /* positioning the background image, aligning it,⏎
 to the top and center */
 background-attachment: fixed; /* making sure the background stays locked in that⏎
 position  */
 background-repeat: no-repeat; /* means you do not wish the background to be repeated */
```

13. Notice the URL address sites.google.com/site/theperfectlandscape/ Background.jpg. That is the image stored in Google Sites. Replace that line of code with the URL of your image.

    When the link is originally pasted, it looks like this:

```
http://sites.google.com/site/theperfectlandscape/Background.jpg?attredirects=0. Be sure
to remove the "attredirects=0."
```

14. Click Save Template.

15. Click View Blog (see Figure 7-8).

Figure 7-8. Custom background installed

The coloring of the post titles and hyperlinks changed to orange and blue. This happened when we changed to the Minima template. Go to Design, then Template Designer, and Advanced to change the colors to match the colors of your new background and banner. In The Perfect Landscape example, the Post Title, Visited Link Color, and Link Color were made green to match the "lawn" appearance of the background and overall landscaping theme.

Convert to a Three-Column Format

Our next step is adding another sidebar (a left sidebar) to convert your blog to a three-column format. You can do this so your sidebar doesn't become overly cluttered. A second sidebar may balance your blog layout. Do not be confused with the three column layout you used back in Chapter 3. That was specifically to be used with templates selected from the Template Designer, not to be used with a custom installation.

Other bloggers use an additional sidebar to keep their gadgets better organized, including keeping ads or buttons to other blogs or sites they like on one side of the blog and more personal information like About Me, contact information, their picture, subscription area, or a gallery on the other. Some bloggers choose not to add another column in order to leave more room for posting.

Although there is a lot of code in the next exercise, I have placed comments next to all the code you will be changing or adding. Again, you are not expected to understand CSS code or be a CSS expert. However, you will be able to change the layout of your blog by following the steps below.

Exercise—Convert to a Three-Column Format

In this exercise, you will be modifying a lot of code and adding some in a few places. It will all be noted and outlined below. Just follow it step by step:

1. Go to Edit HTML.

2. Click Download Full Template.

3. Save the file to your computer. This will serve as a backup in case you have problems with the revisions.

4. Let's get started. The code I have changed or added is bolded, such as the 920px in the second line of code below. I have placed comments throughout the code, denoted between the /* and */ symbols. In addition, those comments can be added to your code as it is properly formatted CSS code.

```
#header-wrapper {
width:920px; /*setting the width of the header area to be 920 pixels*/
margin:0 auto 10px;
border:0px solid #FFFFFF;  /*hiding the border around the header, banner image by⤸
 setting it to 0 or you could have simply delete this entire line.*/
}

#header {
margin: 5px;
border: 0px solid #FFFFFF;  /*hiding the border around the inner part of the header,⤸
 banner image by setting it to 0 or you could simply delete this entire line.*/
text-align: center;
color:#441C1D;
}

#header .description {
margin:0 5px 5px;
padding:0 20px 15px;
max-width:920px; /*setting the width of the header area to be 920 pixels*/
text-transform:uppercase;
letter-spacing:.2em;
line-height: 1.4em;
font: normal normal 78% Verdana, sans-serif;
color: #6F8694;
}

#outer-wrapper {
width: 920px; /*setting the width of the header area to be 920 pixels*/
margin:0 auto;
padding:0px; /* sets the extra space, padding, to 0 meaning there is no padding here */
border-top: 1px solid #000000; ⤸
/* adding a border, to the top, 1 pixel in weight, solid line, black.⤸
 The 000000 is the hexadecimal code for black where FFFFFF is for white*/
border-bottom: 1px solid #000000; /* same as above */
```

```
border-right: 1px solid #000000; /* same as above */
border-left: 1px solid #000000; /* same as above */
text-align:left;
font: normal normal 100% Verdana, sans-serif;
}

/* entire section has been added to create the left column, the new column*/
#left-sidebar-wrapper {    /*name of the column */
width: 200px;  /* width for the column */
float: left;  /* to keep the column on the left side */
padding: 10px;
/* to provide space between the left sidebar and the outer border, otherwise the text↵
 in the left sidebar would be right up against the border with no spacing */
border-top: 1px solid #000000;
/* same as above in regards to the black border being added */
word-wrap: break-word;  /* fix for long text breaking sidebar float in IE */
overflow: hidden;  /* fix for long non-text content breaking IE sidebar float */
}

#main-wrapper {
width: 438px;  /* set the width */
float: left;
padding: 20px;  /* set the padding so the main post area is not flush against the↵
 sidebars */
border-top: 1px solid #000000;
 /* same as above in regards to the black border being added */
border-bottom: 1px solid #000000;
 /* same as above in regards to the black border being added but to the bottom */
border-right: 1px solid #000000;
 /* same as above in regards to the black border being added but to the right */
/border-left: 1px solid #000000;
/* same as above in regards to the black border being added but to the left */
word-wrap: break-word; /* fix for long text breaking sidebar float in IE */
overflow: hidden;     /* fix for long non-text content breaking IE sidebar float */
}

#sidebar-wrapper {
width: 200px; /* set the width of the right column */
float: right;
padding: 10px;
 /* add padding to the right column to allow spacing between the column and the↵
 border */
border-top: 1px solid #000000;
word-wrap: break-word; /* fix for long text breaking sidebar float in IE */
overflow: hidden;     /* fix for long non-text content breaking IE sidebar float */
}
```

5. There is still more. Scroll through the code until you get to the Posts area of the code. Look for /*Posts.

```
.post img {
padding:4px;
border:0px solid #6F8694;
/* this will ensure that no border is place around images in the post area or you↵
 could simply delete this entire line.*/
}
```

6. Scroll to the /*Footer area and set the width to match the header and outer-wrapper areas (920 pixels were used).

```
#footer {
width:920px;   /*setting the width of the footer area to be 920 pixels*/
clear:both;
margin:0 auto;
padding-top:15px;
line-height: 1.6em;
text-transform:uppercase;
letter-spacing:.1em;
text-align: center;
}
```

7. There's one more piece of code that completes the addition of the left sidebar and completes the three-column format conversion.

8. This next section of code is added to install the Blogger Logo gadget in the left sidebar (see Figure 7-9 to view the newly added gadget in the Page Elements screen). You can leave it or remove it.

```
/* this code is adding the Blogger Logo as a Page Element in your new left sidebar */
<div id='left-sidebar-wrapper'>
<b:section class='sidebar' id='left-sidebar' preferred='yes'>
<b:widget id='BloggerButton1' locked='false' title='' type='BloggerButton'/>
</b:section>
</div>
```

Figure 7-9. *Logo Gadget added to left sidebar*

9. The new code is to be added directly above this code:

```
<div id='main-wrapper'>
      <b:section class='main' id='main' showaddelement='no'>
<b:widget id='Blog1' locked='true' title='Blog Posts' type='Blog'/>
</b:section>
      </div>
```

10. It will read as follows:

```
/* this code is adding the Blogger Logo as a Page Element in your new left sidebar */
<div id='left-sidebar-wrapper'>
<b:section class='sidebar' id='left-sidebar' preferred='yes'>
<b:widget id='BloggerButton1' locked='false' title='' type='BloggerButton'/>
</b:section>
</div>

<div id='main-wrapper'>
      <b:section class='main' id='main' showaddelement='no'>
<b:widget id='Blog1' locked='true' title='Blog Posts' type='Blog'/>
</b:section>
      </div>
```

11. Click Save Template.

12. Click View Blog to view your changes (see Figure 7-10 to view The Perfect Landscape's example).

Figure 7-10. Blog converted to a three-column layout

The 920 pixels width setting was used because the banner for The Perfect Landscape had been resized to 900 pixels wide. The extra 20 pixels allows for extra space around the banner image (see Figure 7-10). You can experiment with the settings as desired. Keep in mind that if you reduce the width of the outer wrapper, reduce the left-sidebar wrapper, main wrapper, or sidebar wrapper to accommodate the change. For example, if you change the 920 to 900, reduce the main wrapper (where the posts go) from 438 to 418.

The header wrapper, header description, outer wrapper, and footer should all have the same width as a general rule of thumb.

■ **Note** There are a few sites providing instruction on how to convert your blog to a three-column format. I recommend `threecolumnblogger.com` as an additional resource.

In the previous exercise, certain colors were used including #000000, which is the color black in hexadecimal code. Black is used as the border color in The Perfect Landscape's blog example. For your blog, you may want to use a different color for your borders. Go to Design, then Template Designer, then Advanced. Choose a color from the palette and get the color code under Text Color section. Use that hexadecimal code instead of the #000000 (black) used in the exercise. Also, in the exercise I used a border size of five in the main wrapper area. This is why you see the thick black outline (see Figure 7-10). You may not want that thickness, so experiment starting with a size of one.

Now that your blog has three columns (a left and right sidebar as well as the main posting area), go to Page Elements and equally distribute your sidebar items or drag and drop them however you would like them organized. If you want to remove the Blogger Logo gadget, click Edit next to the element named "Logo" in Page Elements and click Remove. Confirm the deletion by clicking OK. Remember to click Save when you're finished.

Customize Your Post Design

We'll continue redesigning your blog's look by adding a graphical separator between each post. Again, this is a cosmetic change and not at all a requirement in order to have a functional blog. It should be a simplistic image as to not take away from the content of your blog, but this could make your blog stand out from the rest.

In the last example, we edited the CSS code. In this next exercise, you will be adding lines of HTML code and will again use an image loaded to Google Sites. See the exercise named Uploading an Image to Google Sites from Chapter 6 for a refresher on how to upload the image you want to use as your post separator (although brief instructions will be provided in the following exercise).

■ **Note** When creating or purchasing an image to use as your post separator, make sure it is not larger than the posting area (the width of the main wrapper, which in this example is 438px).

Exercise—Installing a Post Separator

As in the previous chapter, you will be uploading an image to Google Sites. It will be used to separate your posts, such as the black scroll (see Figure 7-11). In The Perfect Landscape example, the image used is 338px wide by 50px high. It will be centered at the bottom of each post:

1. Go to `sites.google.com` and if necessary, re-enter your password to Sign In. Otherwise, beneath My Sites, click your site's name.

2. Under More Actions, click Manage Site.

3. Click Attachments (on the left) and click the Upload button to upload the image you would like to use to separate your posts.

4. From your Google Sites account, while still viewing your uploaded attachments, right-click the recently uploaded image (post separator) and click Copy Link Location or Copy Shortcut (depending on your Internet browser).

5. Switch to Blogger and go to Edit HTML.

6. Check the box Expand Widgets.

7. Using the keyboard shortcuts (CTRL + F), find `post-footer-line-3`.

8. You will be inserting the bolded code below, centering the image referenced from Google Sites.

```
<div class='post-footer-line post-footer-line-3'><span class='post-location'>
<b:if cond='data:top.showLocation'>
<b:if cond='data:post.location'>
<data:postLocationLabel/>
<a expr:href='data:post.location.mapsUrl' target='_blank'><data:post.location.name/></a>
</b:if>
</b:if>
</span>
<div align='center'>
<img src='http://sites.google.com/site/theperfectlandscape/post-seperator.jpg'/>
</div>
</div>
```

9. Paste your link from Google Sites and modify it, removing question marks and the code afterward. For example, this link:

```
http://sites.google.com/site/theperfectlandscape/post-seperator.jpg?attredirects=0
```

becomes:

```
http://sites.google.com/site/theperfectlandscape/post-seperator.jpg
```

10. Save and view your blog (see Figure 7-11).

Figure 7-11. Post separator installed

121

Using a Background Image in Your Sidebar

Let's continue with your blog's makeover by installing an image that will appear in the background of each sidebar title. You will upload this image to your Google Sites account as previously done. It should be a relatively small image since it needs to fit in your sidebar and not overlap your sidebar headings.

Exercise—Using a Background Image in Your Sidebar

In this example, I used a small image (22px by 20px). It will be placed to the left of the sidebar heading and centered vertically as well:

1. From your Google Sites account, while still viewing your uploaded attachments, right-click the image you want to use as your sidebar background and click Copy Link Location or Copy Shortcut (depending on your Internet browser).

2. In Blogger, go to Edit HTML. You will be adding CSS code to format the sidebar heading title area.

3. Scroll or find the following line of code:

```
/* Sidebar Content
--------------------------------------------- */
```

4. Underneath that line of code, paste the code you'll find below replacing the highlighted (bolded) URL with your own from Google Sites.

```
.sidebar h2 {
background: url(http://sites.google.com/site/theperfectlandscape/sidebar-background.jpg)
no-repeat center left;
padding:.2em 0;
text-indent: 30px;   /* this indents the text in your sidebar title so it doesn't overlap
the image and become hard to read*/
}
```

5. Save and view your blog (see Figure 7-12).

Figure 7-12. Background image in sidebar headings

So, how many cups of coffee did you have? You've made it through the advanced design techniques! I hope you enjoy your new, customized blog design. See Chapter 9 for image size guidelines and other helpful tips in preparing for future blog enhancements, and also if you want to continue experimenting.

Summary

We covered a lot in this chapter in regard to customizing and personalizing the look of your blog. First, we experimented with free Blogger templates from The Cutest Blog on the Block, eBlog Templates, and Blogger Templates Free. Next, through a series of exercises, you learned how to manually change your blog's design using CSS and HTML code.

Although there are many professional free templates available on the Internet, there may come a time you to change your layout by installing custom made images or making changes like adding borders to the columns or adjusting the padding (spacing) as we just did. In the next chapter, you will take your blog layout to the next level by learning how to set up pages, create an online blog store, and insert a navigational bar (menu bar).

CHAPTER 8

■ ■ ■

Setting Up a Blog Store

In addition to using your blog to share information with your readers and keeping them informed of promotions or upcoming events via posts, you can use your blog to sell products or services you offer. Although I would recommend you create a post about a new product or service so people who subscribe to your blog will be updated as soon as possible, I would also recommend having a page set up listing all your products and services. This allows your readers to quickly and easily access all your products or services without having to search your blog.

In Chapter 2, you created a post. In this chapter, you will create pages. What's the difference between a post and a page? A post is information (text, images, video, etc.) you publish to your blog to share with blog visitors. When you post, your subscribers will be updated automatically.

A page is similar to a post in its creation and layout. However, there is one major difference: Blog subscribers are not informed if a page is published. Blogger has a Pages gadget that can be added to your blog and located in your blog's sidebar or in the header area, preferably under your banner. If added in the header area, it serves as a navigation or menu bar.

The Pages gadget allows your visitors access to your pages. In the upcoming exercises, you will create the following pages and in doing so, you will have a better understanding of the use and purpose of pages:

- About Me

- Services

- Products

You may also want to create pages for Contact Me or Testimonials. A little homework!

Furthermore, creating pages is the first step in setting up your blog store. In creating the Services and Products pages, you will learn how to use Google Checkout and PayPal to accept payments online. While we will review both methods (Google Checkout and PayPal), choose one to use consistently throughout your blog.

In the last chapter, I mentioned getting a cup of coffee before starting. Here, I think you may want to bring out the espresso . . . make it a double espresso!

Creating Pages

Let's begin with creating an About Me page. This is a page about yourself or your business, or a brief biography or business history (how and when the business was started, its mission and purpose, or benefits). An About Me page or informational page is not updated frequently. It would not change daily or even monthly, but maybe once or twice a year.

Exercise—Creating a Page and Adding the Pages Gadget

In the next exercise, you will create an About Me page and add the Pages gadget to your blog for easy access and to serve as menu. You can use Pages to create a textual navigational bar under your banner:

1. Log in to Blogger.

2. From your Dashboard, click Edit Posts.

3. Click Edit Pages.

4. You can click New Page, which brings up the Pages Editor (see Figure 8-1). It looks similar to the Post Editor you have been using thus far to compose and publish posts.

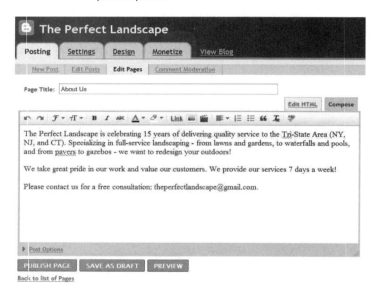

Figure 8-1. Create a new page

5. In my example, I used About Us as the Page Title, but you may use About Me or About.

6. Begin writing your content just as you would if you were creating a new post. The toolbar is the same. You can still format your text, insert images, etc. Anything you can do with a post, you can do here when creating a page.

7. When complete, click Publish Page and you will be prompted with "How would you like the Pages Gadget to appear?" (See Figure 8-2).

a. If you want to add a quick navigational bar (or menu) to your blog, choose Blog Tabs (see Figure 8-2).

b. If you prefer to have the links to your pages appear in a list on the sidebar, choose Blog Sidebar.

c. At this point, I would not recommend the No Gadget option. Your blog visitors will not have a way of accessing your Pages (without manually having to create a Links List or write HTML code using the HTML/JavaScript gadget).

Figure 8-2. Adding the Pages gadget

8. In this example, choose Blog Tabs.

9. Click Save and Publish.

10. You will receive a message that the page was published successfully.

11. Click View Page to view your new page (see Figure 8-3 to view the new menu bar under the banner which has Home and About Us in my example for The Perfect Landscape). Figure 8-3 also shows the About Us page I created. It is similar to a post but is missing the Date Header. Other than that, it has the same formatting, look, and feel of a post.

Figure 8-3. View new page and menu

12. Click the Back button on your Internet browser and you're back at Page Elements (where you see a visual layout of all gadgets added to your blog in the header, sidebars, and footer areas). The newly added Pages gadget has been added beneath the header (banner) area.

We will revisit the Pages Gadget after we've created more pages. We'll then review the different options and how you can rearrange page order on your menu bar or sidebar list.

Next, we'll create a page listing your services. In The Perfect Landscape example, we will use landscaping services such as lawn cuts and garden beds.

Exercise—Creating a Services Page

If you clicked View Blog and then used the Back button on your browser, click the Dashboard, Edit Posts, and Edit Pages. If you did not click View Blog and are viewing the "Your page was published successfully!" message, click Edit Posts and Edit Pages.

1. When you click Edit Pages, your About Us page is listed. Click New Page.

2. In Page Title (for this example), click Services.

3. Enter a brief explanation of services you offer and begin creating your list of services (see Figure 8-4). Although our example is for landscaping services, you can customize it to suit your business or blog purpose.

4. Click Publish Page to save your work.

5. You will receive the message that your page has been created successfully. There is an Edit Page link. We will revisit this page shortly when the payment buttons are added.

I am separating the process of creating the page and Google Checkout registration. You've just completed the Services page. In the next exercise, you will create a Google Checkout account, and then create the buttons needed to allow visitors to pay for the services listed.

Using Google Checkout

Now that your Services page is created, you will add payment buttons under each service allowing your customers to pay online using Google Checkout.

Google Checkout is a fast and secure type of online merchant account (an account processing online payment transactions) allowing your customers and blog visitors to make a payment online from your blog with ease and confidence.

In the remaining exercises in this book (beginning with the next exercise), you will switch regularly between Blogger and Google Checkout (and later between Blogger and PayPal). You will have at least two Internet browser windows open; one with Blogger and one with Google Checkout or PayPal.

Figure 8-4. Sample services page

Exercise—Setting Up Google Checkout

1. In this exercise you will be setting up a Google Checkout account. To begin, open a new browser window.

2. Go to checkout.google.com/sell/.

3. On the right, log in using your Google account (enter your existing Blogger password).

4. Click Sign In and Continue. You'll see a screen (see Figure 8-5).

Figure 8-5. Google Checkout sign in

5. Because you already have a Google Account, choose the first option under "Would you like to have a single account for all Google Services" stating "Yes, we'd like to use our existing Google Account for Google Checkout."

6. Re-enter your password and click "Sign In and Continue."

7. In the next screen (see Figure 8-6), there are fields for you to enter information about your business.

a. Private Contact Information: Your name, address, phone and number in order for Google to get in touch with you.

b. Public Contact Information: Contact information for your customers to contact you (business name, email address, web site/blog URL, business address, business type, and what name or text you would like to appear on your customer's payment receipt).

c. Financial Information: Information about your sales volume and credit information.

d. Terms of Service: Please read before checking that you agree to Google Checkout's terms of service.

Figure 8-6. *Tell Us About Your Business (Google Checkout)*

8. Click Complete Sign Up.

9. You will see "Sign up complete" and a type of menu for what to do next (see Figure 8-7).

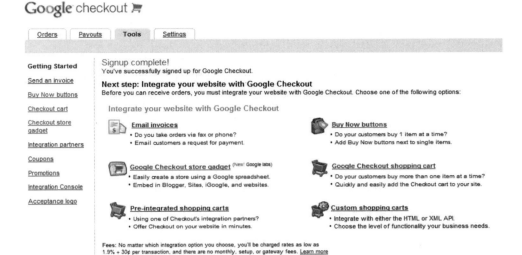

Figure 8-7. Integrate your web site with Google Checkout

> In the next exercise, you will continue with Google Checkout and adding buttons to your Services page. You will be toggling between Blogger and Google Checkout.

Now that you have created a Google Checkout account and saved the Services page (in Blogger), it is time to integrate. You will add the payment buttons to your blog in the following exercise. There are two types of buttons including Add to Cart and Buy Now. The Add to Cart button is more popular, so we will install it first. It allows purchasers to pay for more than one service or product before checking out. This normally increases your sales because customers can do their shopping at once without having to do separate transactions for each item.

Exercise—Adding Payment Buttons to the Services Page

At this point, you have at least two Internet windows open; a Blogger window where you are viewing a message that the Services page was published successfully, and Google Checkout where you have just completed registration (see Figure 8-7):

1. Click Google Checkout Shopping Carts (see Figure 8-8).

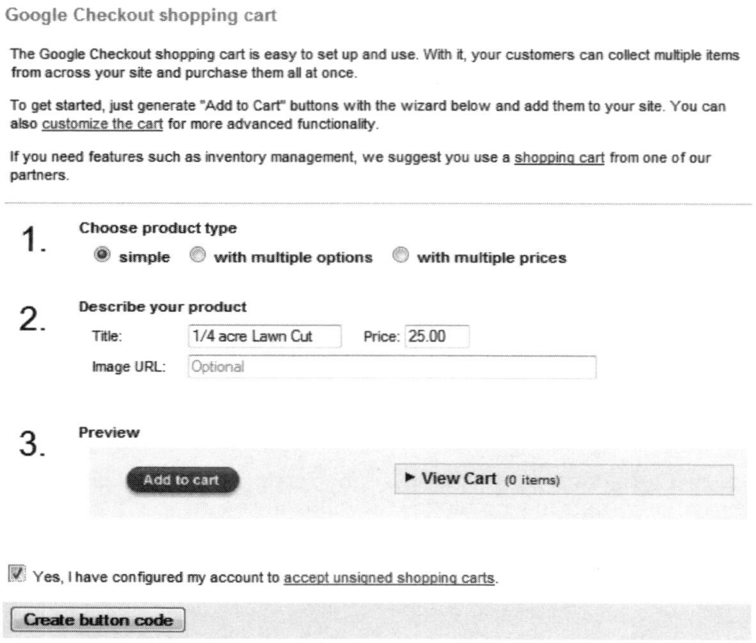

Google Checkout shopping cart

The Google Checkout shopping cart is easy to set up and use. With it, your customers can collect multiple items from across your site and purchase them all at once.

To get started, just generate "Add to Cart" buttons with the wizard below and add them to your site. You can also customize the cart for more advanced functionality.

If you need features such as inventory management, we suggest you use a shopping cart from one of our partners.

1. Choose product type
   ⦿ simple ○ with multiple options ○ with multiple prices

2. Describe your product
   Title: [1/4 acre Lawn Cut]   Price: [25.00]
   Image URL: [Optional]

3. Preview

   (Add to cart)   ► View Cart (0 items)

☑ Yes, I have configured my account to accept unsigned shopping carts.

[Create button code]

Figure 8-8. Google Checkout shopping cart

2. In the Shopping Cart, choose Product Type. For this example, Simple is selected. The "With multiple options" or "With multiple prices" are used to configure a drop-down box. This could be used if you had different sizes of the same product that you want to sell, and therefore different prices based on the size.

3. In the Describe Your Product section, enter the Title (description of your product or service) and Price. Leave Image URL blank. You will not be entering images for your product/service using this method. Instead, we've listed services in the Services page. If you were selling a product, you would insert the image directly in the page, not here.

4. Check the box that says you are allowing unsigned shopping carts (this will allow transactions that don't have a digital signature, which the majority of your customers will not have). Be sure to check this box.

5. Click Create Button Code.

6. You will be shown two boxes of code (see Figure 8-9); each needs to be added to your blog.

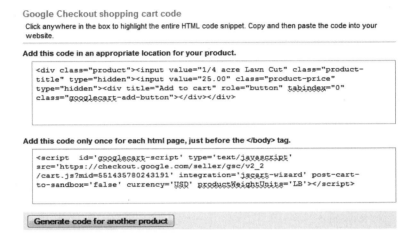

Figure 8-9. *Google Checkout button code*

7. Select the code in the first box and copy it.

8. Switch to Blogger. Click Edit page to edit the Services page.

9. Click the Edit HTML tab within the Page Editor (under and to the right of the Title). At this point, your page does not look "pretty," but instead is composed of HTML tags and text (see Figure 8-10).

Figure 8-10. Edit HTML within the Services Page

10. Scroll through the code to find your first service (in our example, it's the ¼ Acre Lawn Cut) and paste the code under the service (see Figure 8-10).

11. Click on the Compose tab to view the "normal" view of your page without the HTML tags. Although you have just copied and pasted code from Google Checkout, you do not see the button yet. This is okay.

12. Click Publish Page.

13. Only once, you now need to copy the code in the second box from Google Checkout.

14. Switch to Google Checkout. Copy the code in the second box.

15. Switch to Blogger. Click Design.

16. Click Edit HTML (here, you are editing your blog's template, not that of a specific page).

17. You must paste this code toward the bottom of your template code right above the `<body>` tag (see Figure 8-11).

Edit Template

Edit the contents of your template. Learn more

☐ Expand Widget Templates

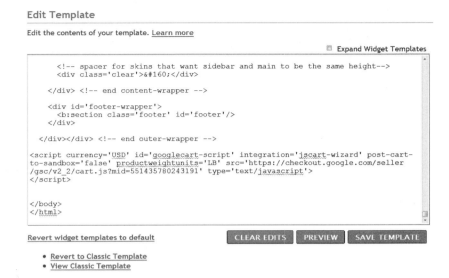

```
      <!-- spacer for skins that want sidebar and main to be the same height-->
      <div class='clear'> </div>

   </div> <!-- end content-wrapper -->

   <div id='footer-wrapper'>
      <b:section class='footer' id='footer'/>
   </div>

  </div></div> <!-- end outer-wrapper -->

<script currency='USD' id='googlecart-script' integration='jscart-wizard' post-cart-
to-sandbox='false' productweightunits='LB' src='https://checkout.google.com/seller
/gsc/v2_2/cart.js?mid=551435780243191' type='text/javascript'>
</script>


</body>
</html>
```

Revert widget templates to default   [CLEAR EDITS] [PREVIEW] [SAVE TEMPLATE]

- Revert to Classic Template
- View Classic Template

Figure 8-11. Edit HTML within layout

18. Click Save Changes. Again, you only have to do this part once although you will now be creating additional Add to Cart buttons.

19. Switch to Google Checkout. Click Generate Code for Another Product.

20. In my example, I changed the Title to read "1/2 Acre Lawn Cut," the price to "$50.00," and clicked Create Button Code.

21. Although you again see two text boxes of code, only use the top box.

22. Select and copy all of the code from the top where it says "Add this code in an appropriate location for your product."

23. Switch to Blogger. Click Posting and Edit Pages. Click OK.

24. You will see a list of your pages (About Us and Services are the only two you've create this far). Click Edit under Services.

25. Click Edit HTML (you are editing the HTML code in the Service page).

26. Scroll through the code and look for text describing your second product (or service). In our example, it is "½ Acre Lawn Cut."

27. Paste the code from the top box in Google Checkout.

28. Click Publish Page and View Page. You can see both buttons when viewing in your Internet browser, although they are not seen in the Compose view of your page.

29. Click the Back button on your browser.

30. Click Edit Page.

31. Continue this process until you have added all the Add to Cart buttons for your products or services (switching back and forth between Google Checkout and Blogger).

    a.   Go back to Google and click Generate Code for Another Product.

    b.   Select and copy the code in the top box.

    c.   Switch back to your Services page in Blogger.

    d.   Go to Edit HTML in that Page finding your next product (or service) and pasting the code.

At the end of the exercise, you should have Add to Cart buttons for all of your products or services for sale (see Figure 8-12).

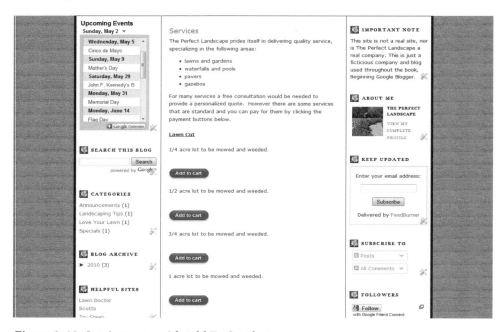

Figure 8-12. Services page with Add To Cart buttons

In the next exercise you will install a Buy Now button. Using a Buy Now button allows you the ability to include a link to a PDF or other document or file that the purchaser would be directed to upon payment. This could be a good option if you are selling an eBook or other type of online document, or if you would like to send a customized receipt or "thank you" note. This option is not required and you can create the button for payment only.

Exercise—Adding a Buy Now Button in Google Checkout

In this exercise, using The Perfect Landscape example, there will be a Buy Now button for the eBook added to the bottom of the Services Page:

1. Starting in Blogger, edit the Services page to include a new item for sale. I included a picture of an eBook as an example at the bottom of the page. Enter the title beneath it and the price. The Buy Now button will be inserted beneath the price.

2. Switch to Google Checkout. On the left, click Buy Now buttons (see Figure 8-13 appears).

Figure 8-13. Create a Buy Now button

3. Choose a button type. I used Basic, however if you had multiple options (including different prices for different formats of the book), you would use Buttons With Options.

4. Choose a Button Style. Use "My website has a white background" or the other button otherwise. In our example, The Perfect Landscape has a white background main posting area (see Figure 8-13).

5. In the Describe Your Button area, choose Shipped Item or Digital Download. In this example, Digital Download is selected. Therefore, you have the additional fields of entering a Key, URL, and Instructions.

6. Enter the Item Name.

7. Enter a Description (if desired).

8. Enter the Price.

9. In the URL field, I copied and pasted the link to the PDF for the eBook. Again, this means your customers will be directed to this link upon payment. You may also enter a Key if you want it to be password-protected. You may add additional instructions to the purchaser. If you are using the link to send your customers a customized "thank you" note, it must be stored online. Many use Google Docs for online document storage. Visit docs.google.com for more information.

10. Click Create Button Code.

11. A box will appear below the Create Button Code containing the HTML for your new button.

12. Select the code and copy it.

13. Switch to Blogger. Go back to edit your Services pages. Click Posts, Edit Posts, and Edit Pages). Click Edit beneath the Services page.

14. Click Edit HTML.

15. Scroll to the bottom of your page (beneath the new eBook item you added).

16. Press Enter on your keyboard.

17. Paste the HTML code you just copied.

18. Switch back to Compose view.

19. Click Publish Page.

20. Click View Page. Blogger adds spacing above these types of buttons (see Figure 8-14).

We have a book!

Redesigning Your Life Through Your Outdoors
Price: $9.95
(Electronic version only - PDF Format)

Figure 8-14. *Spacing above Buy Now Button shown*

21. To remove the extra spacing you can only modify the inserted HTML code. Be very careful not to delete necessary code to make the button work.

22. Switch to Edit HTML.

23. Scroll to the bottom to view the newly inserted code shown here:

```
<div style="text-align: center;">
<form action="https://checkout.google.com/api/checkout/v2/checkoutForm/Merchant↵
/551435780243191" id="BB_BuyButtonForm" method="post" name="BB_BuyButtonForm"↵
 target="_top">
<input name="item_name_1" type="hidden" value="The Perfect Landscape e-Book" />
<input name="item_description_1" type="hidden" value="Redesigning your life through↵
 your outdoors!" />
<input name="item_quantity_1" type="hidden" value="1" />
<input name="item_price_1" type="hidden" value="9.95" />
<input name="item_currency_1" type="hidden" value="USD" />
<input name="shopping-cart.items.item-1.digital-content.url" type="hidden" value=↵
"https://docs.google.com/fileview?id=0B0tc5eGgfh1jODVkYzFkMzUtM2U1YS0oOTIwLWIxODMtND↵
kON2NiMzExZjBm&amp;hl=en" />
<input name="_charset_" type="hidden" value="utf-8" />
<input alt="" src="https://checkout.google.com/buttons/buy.gif?merchant_id=↵
551435780243191&amp;w=117&amp;h=48&amp;style=white&amp;variant=text&amp;loc↵
=en_US" type="image" /></form>
</div>
```

24. Modify it to resemble the code below (where I went to the end of many lines and pressed the Delete key to reduce the number of hard returns). The resulting code will look crammed, however it is okay and will display properly when viewed in a browser.

```
<div style="text-align: center;">
<form action="https://checkout.google.com/api/checkout/v2/checkoutForm/Merchant/↵
551435780243191" id="BB_BuyButtonForm" method="post" name="BB_BuyButtonForm"↵
 target="_top"><input name="item_name_1" type="hidden" value="The Perfect Landscape↵
 e-Book" /><input name="item_description_1" type="hidden" value="Redesigning your life↵
 through your outdoors!" /><input name="item_quantity_1" type="hidden" value="1" />
<input name="item_price_1" type="hidden" value="9.95" /><input name="item_currency_1"↵
 type="hidden" value="USD" /><input name="shopping-cart.items.item-1.digital-↵
content.url" type="hidden" value=↵
"https://docs.google.com/fileview?id=0B0tc5eGgfh1jODVkYzFkMzUtM2U1YS0o0TIwLWIx0↵
DMtNDkON2NiMzExZjBm&amp;hl=en" /><input name="_charset_" type="hidden"↵
 value="utf-8" /><input alt="" src="https://checkout.google.com/buttons/buy.gif?↵
merchant_id=551435780243191&amp;w=117&amp;h=48&amp;style=white&amp;variant=↵
text&amp;loc=en_US" type="image" /></form>
</div>
```

25. Click Publish Page and View Page again. The spacing above the button is reduced (see Figure 8-15).

We have a book!

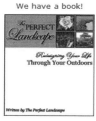

Redesigning Your Life Through Your Outdoors
Price: $9.95
(Electronic version only - PDF Format)

Figure 8-15. *Spacing removed*

We are now done with the Services Page and using Google Checkout. You now know how to create Add to Cart and Buy Now buttons, so you may use both to suit your specific business or personal needs.

When a blog visitor clicks your Google Checkout buttons, a View Cart window appears in the upper-right corner of your screen (see Figure 8-16) listing the items added to the cart. They can continue to checkout by clicking the Google Checkout button.

Figure 8-16. Google Checkout view cart

Using PayPal

PayPal is a popular service, like Google Checkout, allowing you to receive online payments. Purchasers may pay using their PayPal account or using a credit card, which is why many merchants use it. Unlike Google Checkout, purchasers are not required to create a PayPal account when using PayPal payment buttons. You can use PayPal as your online merchant account (credit card processor). However, like a traditional merchant account, PayPal charges you a fee for all online transactions (payments received). The rate can vary from 1.9 percent to 2.9 percent depending on the previous month's sales volume. Although there are fees associated with accepting payments via PayPal, I think you will find the installation of the buttons simpler than Google Checkout for three reasons. You can see the button while in Compose view, there is one area of code to copy and paste from PayPal, and you only need to copy code into the page (not the main Blogger template).

In the next example, you'll create a Products page and use PayPal instead of Google Checkout. The concept is the same and process is similar. However, the use of HTML code in the Products page will be different to better format your page and give it a professional look. You do not have to know HTML to complete this exercise. You can copy and paste the code from this book's source code library or manually type it. If you are not comfortable experimenting with HTML, skip the part of the exercise when creating the HTML Table and instead list the items as you did in the Services page.

Exercise—Creating a Products Page

Similarly to what you did with the Services page, you will create a Products page. However, here I detail an advanced way to display your products for sale in a table format (see Figure 8-17).

Products

We highly recommend the following products and use them in business and for our personal landscaping needs. You may purchase these products from us at cost but will have to pay for shipping which will be calculated at checkout based on weight (U.S. Sales only).

Figure 8-17. Products Page Table

1. If you are not already in the Pages area of Blogger, click Posts, Edit Posts, and Edit Pages. Click New Page.

2. Enter a Title (Products for example).

3. Enter a brief introduction to your store page if you'd like (see Figure 8-17).

4. Click Edit HTML (to edit the HTML code for the Products page only).

5. Under the introduction, copy and paste this code from the source code library or type it into your page:

```
<TABLE align="center" cellpadding="10">
<TR>
<TD valign=bottom>Item Name<BR>Description<BR>Price<BR></TD>
```

```
<TD valign=bottom >Item Name<BR>Description<BR>Price<BR></TD>
<TD valign=bottom >Item Name<BR>Description<BR>Price<BR></TD>
</TR>
<TR>
<TD valign=bottom >Item Name<BR>Description<BR>Price<BR></TD>
<TD valign=bottom >Item Name<BR>Description<BR>Price<BR></TD>
<TD valign=bottom >Item Name<BR>Description<BR>Price<BR></TD>
</TR></TABLE>
```

6. What does this mean? This is a table in HTML code. Give this a try. If it doesn't work out for you and you have too much trouble editing it later in the exercise, go back to what is comfortable and familiar: create a list like you did for Services.

7. There is the table tag `<TABLE align="center" cellpadding="10")>…</TABLE>`. This says there is a table centered on the page and each item in the table has 10 spaces between it (so they are not too crowded).

8. It contains two rows (denoted with two sets of `<TR>…</TR>`) and three columns (denoted by the three sets of `<TD>…</TD>`). The column items are aligned vertically to the bottom (this will keep your store items in line regardless of the height or width of each item picture). The `<BR>` is a line break (as if you pressed the Enter key).

9. If you were to Publish Page and View Page at this point, it would look like Figure 8-18.

Below is a list of products we highly recommend and sell at cost (plus shipping).

Item Name	Item Name	Item Name
Description	Description	Description
Price	Price	Price
Item Name	Item Name	Item Name
Description	Description	Description
Price	Price	Price

SHARE |

LINKS TO THIS POST

Figure 8-18. Products Page table set up

10. Now compare Figures 8-17 and 8-18. For "Item Name" I inserted a picture. In Description, the name/description of the item. And then entered the price.

11. At this point, you have already inserted in the code in Edit HTML. Now click on Compose to view your page (see Figure 8-18).

12. Highlight the words Item Name.

13. From the toolbar, click on the Insert Image button (see Figure 8-19 which shows you where the Insert Image button is).

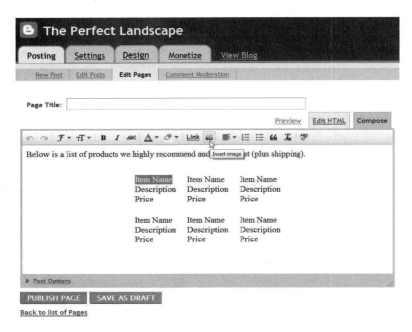

Figure 8-19. *The table before inserting the image*

14. Select an image from your computer for the product you want to list.

15. Once inserted (if too large), click Small from the menu that appears under the inserted image.

16. Select "Description" and enter a description or name.

17. Select "Price" and enter the price of the product.

18. Go to the next item (row one, column two) and insert another image, and enter Description and Price.

19. Do the same for as many items as you need. If you need more than six, copy and paste (or re-enter) the same code listed above at the bottom of the existing HTML code (Edit HTML view) and another six "place holders" will appear (see Figure 8-18). If you don't need all six, delete the text.

20. When finished, click Publish Page.

21. Click View Page (see Figure 8-17).

At this point your page is set up. The items are presented in a table format. Next, you will be adding the PayPal buttons below each item.

I know that exercise was advanced, but I wanted you to have a nicely formatted store page and to learn a different way of listing items without listing them vertically as we did on the Services Page. Now all you have to do is add the Add to Cart buttons.

Note If you want to learn more or want to experiment with HTML Tables, go to w3schools.com/html/html_tables.asp.

Exercise—Setting Up PayPal and Create Add to Cart Buttons

First set up a PayPal account if you don't already have one:

1. From the Google Checkout window, go to PayPal.com to sign up. You now have opened a Blogger window and a PayPal window (instead of Blogger and Google Checkout).

2. Click Get Started under Premier in order to use "selling" capabilities.

3. Enter your information including your email, password, first and last name, date of birth, address, and phone.

4. Click Agree and Continue.

5. Choose how to pay for purchases (even if you don't plan on using it for buying, this step is required).

6. Under Bank Account, click Continue.

7. Click Go To My Account at the bottom left. We will address entering bank information at the end of the exercise. For now, proceed with creating payment buttons.

8. To create a button, go to the Merchant Services tab (see Figure 8-20).

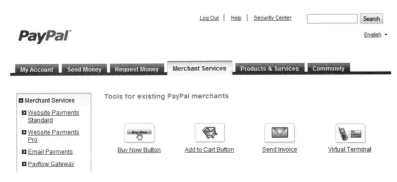

Figure 8-20. *Paypal Merchant Services*

9. Click the Add to Cart button. The form shown in Figure 8-21 appears.

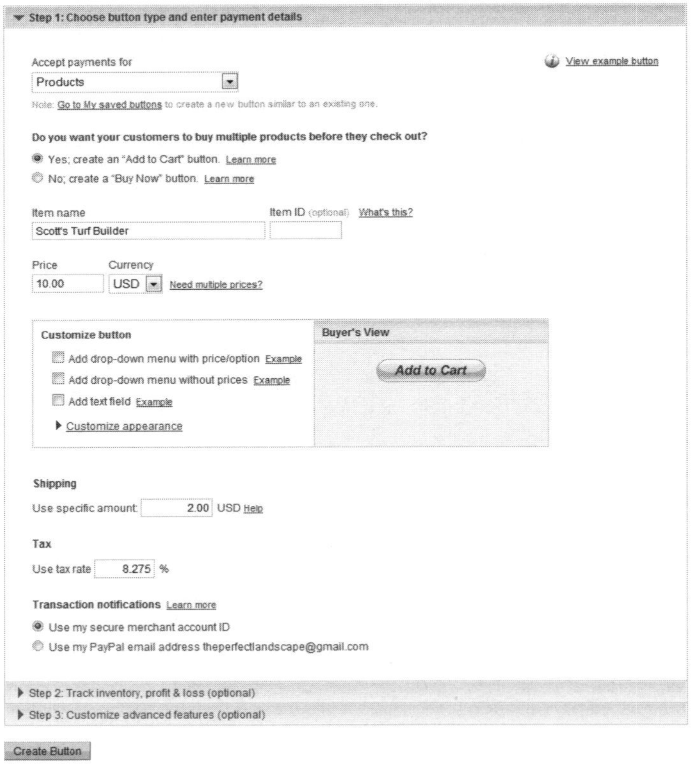

Figure 8-21. *PayPal Add To Cart*

10. The option for "Yes, create an Add to Cart button" should be selected.

11. Enter the Item Name.

12. Do not enter an Item ID (unless you plan on tracking inventory which is not covered in this book).

13. Continue with entering the Price and currency.

14. Enter Shipping amount (if applicable).

15. Enter Tax (if applicable).

16. Click the Create Button (see Figure 8-22).

Figure 8-22. Payal Add to Cart button code

17. Select and copy the code. You may click the Select Code button to select all of the code if you want to be sure you select everything. That code should look like this:

```
<form target="paypal" action="https://www.paypal.com/cgi-bin/webscr" method="post">
<input type="hidden" name="cmd" value="_s-xclick">
<input type="hidden" name="hosted_button_id" value="FEGJ2RE6ALQUN">
<input type="image" src="https://www.paypal.com/en_US/i/btn/btn_cart_LG.gif"↵
 border="0" name="submit" alt="PayPal - The safer, easier way to pay online!">
```

```
<img alt="" border="0" src="https://www.paypal.com/en_US/i/scr/pixel.gif" width=⏎
"1" height="1">
</form>
```

18. Switch to Blogger. Go to the Products page and click Edit Page. If you need to get back to pages, click Posts, Edit Posts, and Edit Pages. Click Edit beneath the Products page.

19. Scroll to where you see the price for the first item (in our example, the Scott's Turf Builder). Below the price, enter <BR> and paste the code.

20. Click Compose view (see Figure 8-23).

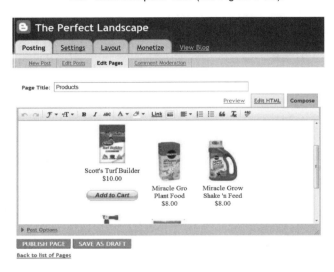

Figure 8-23. Compose view of post with button added

21. Switch to PayPal. Click Create Similar Button to create a button for your next item.

22. Continue steps 11-21 (switching between Blogger and PayPal) until all Add to Cart buttons have been created (see Figure 8-24).

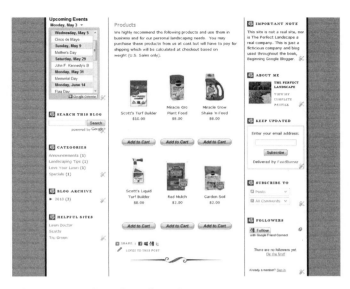

Figure 8-24. View of Products Page

23. After selecting, copying, and pasting the code for the last item, go back to PayPal and click Create a View Cart Button (see Figure 8-25). This will allow visitors to see their shopping cart at any time. Click Create Button. Select and copy the code.

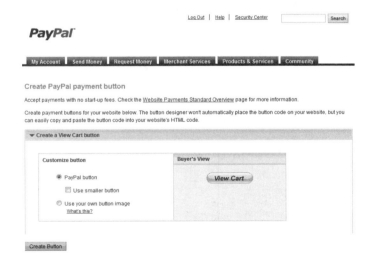

Figure 8-25. Create View Cart button

24. Switch to Blogger. Go to the Products page.

25. Click Edit HTML.

26. Under the introduction of the page, paste the View Cart button code (so it appears before all store items).

27. Click Compose.

28. Click the newly added View Cart button and center it by clicking the Center button on the toolbar.

29. Publish Page and View Page.

You may also set up shipping preferences and tax so you don't manually have to enter them each time (if applicable). Go to the Merchant Services tab, Shipping Calculator, and Shipping Preferences. For tax, go to the Tax Calculator.

To transfer money you receive from PayPal to your bank account, you can set up your Bank Information. Click Profile and under Financial Information, click Bank Accounts, Add Bank, and enter your checking or savings account information.

Hang in there! We are almost done with this section. Next, I want to share with you PayPal's Buy Now button. It is similar to that of Google Checkout, and again we'll experiment with the digital download (directing customers to a PDF file upon payment) like we did on the Services Page. As in the Google Checkout section, we'll again use the eBook example.

Exercise—Adding a PayPal Buy Now Button

In this exercise, you will be adding the eBook item at the very bottom of the Products Page under the table:

1. Begin in Blogger. Go to the Products Page and open it for editing.

2. Click Edit HTML, scroll to the bottom and press the Enter key a few times. Type Enter Item Here.

3. Click Compose View.

4. You can see the eBook will be beneath below the table and will not interfere with its formatting.

5. Select Enter Item Here and insert your image.

6. Enter the Name or Description for the item and below that, the Price.

7. Switch to PayPal. At this point, time has elapsed and you may have to log back into PayPal. This may happen at any time while building your store pages if PayPal has been idle for too long.

8. Go to Merchant Services (see Figure 8-20).

9. Click the Buy Now button (see Figure 8-26 appears).

10. Enter the Item Name and Price. If you need to create a list of different item options and pricing, you could use the Customize Button and check "Add drop-down menu with price option" and enter as many Item Names and Prices as needed.

11. Do not enter shipping for this example since it is a digital download.

12. Enter tax (if applicable).

13. You'll skip Step 2 of this form since we are not tracking inventory in this example. Click Step 3 "Customize Advanced Features (Optional)" (see Figure 8-27).

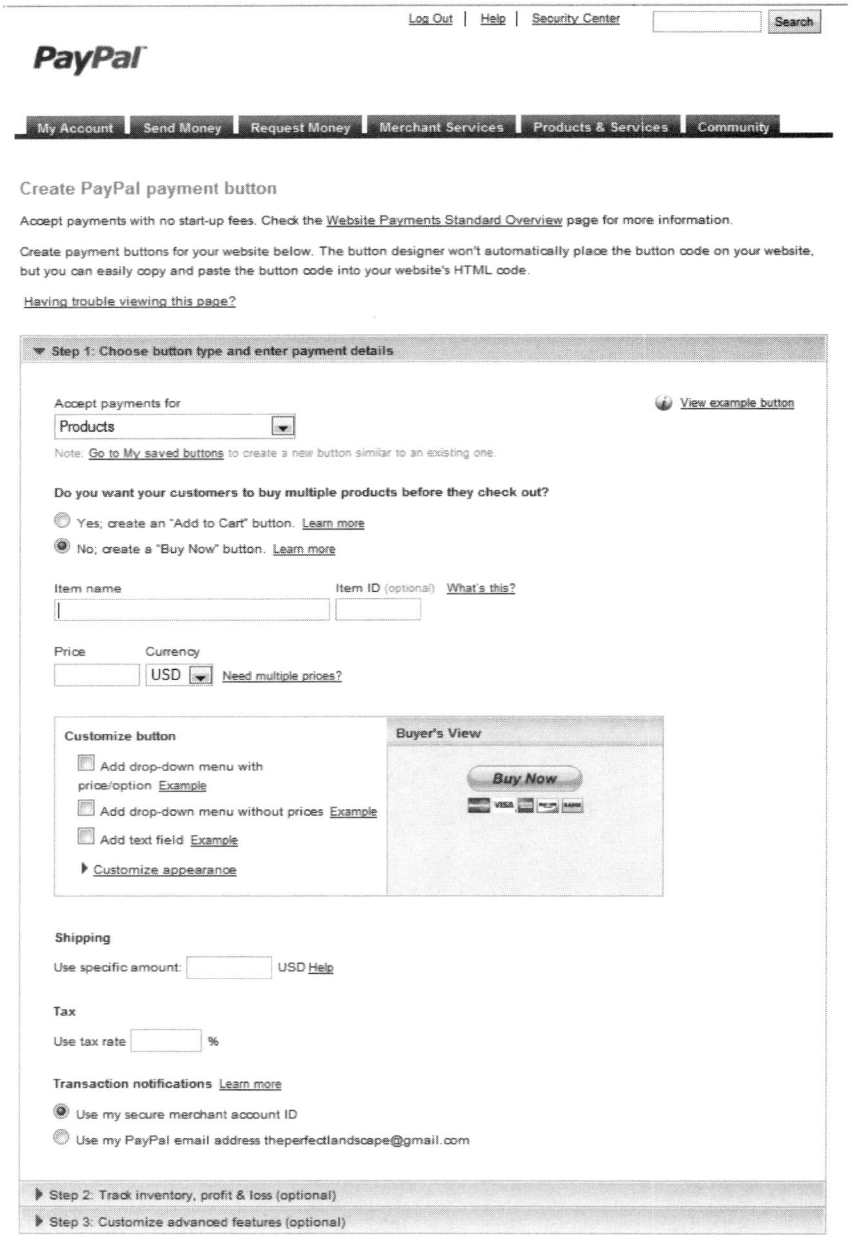

Figure 8-26. *Create Buy Now button*

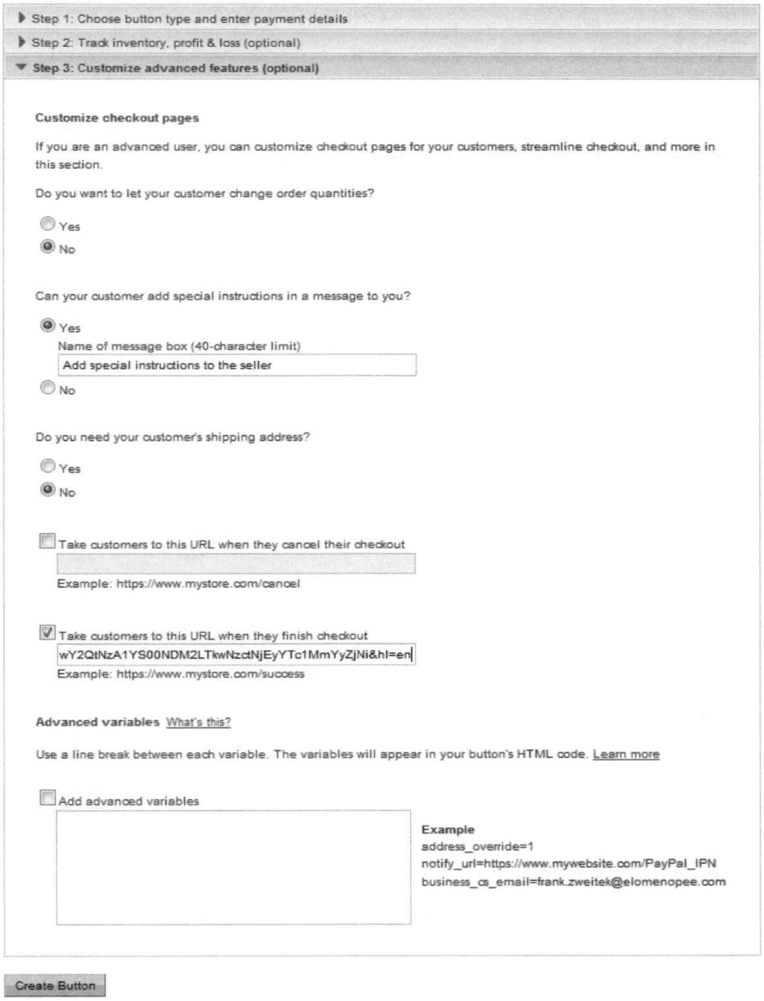

Figure 8-27. Advanced features in PayPal Buy Now button

14. Click No for "Do you need your customer's mailing address" and check "Take customers to this URL when they have finished checkout."

15. Paste the same URL you used previously in the Services Page. As noted in the Services Page example, you may link to any online document. Google Docs is a free service. To learn more, visit docs.google.com.

16. Click the Create button.

17. Select and copy the code provided by PayPal.

18. Switch to Blogger. Go back to your Products page, click Edit HTML and go to the bottom of the page and paste the code (under the price of the eBook (in The Perfect Landscape example).

19. If necessary, you can select the item, description, price, PayPal button, and center it (by using the Align Center button on the toolbar).

20. Click Publish Page.

21. Click View Page.

Now you are done. Congratulations!

Before concluding this chapter, I want to note a significant difference between the Add to Cart and Buy Now buttons. In using Add to Cart buttons, although you can add a link that customers would be directed to after payment, I would recommend all Add to Cart buttons have the same link, such as directing them to a PDF that is a "thank you for your purchase" type of document with a coupon (for example). The links will not work properly if you add different links. PayPal cannot send the customer to multiple links at the same time. That's why I used the Buy Now button with the link option, as it is a one-to-one relationship and works beautifully.

Summary

We began this chapter with a review of pages and how they differ from posts—your blog subscribers are not notified when you create a new page. However, in using pages, you can quickly and easily create a navigational bar or menu allowing visitors to find the information about you, your services, and products offered.

We took that concept to the next level by adding payment options to your Services and Products page through Google Checkout and PayPal respectively. As noted earlier, we used both methods since both are commonly used on blogs and web sites to allow online transactions. However, it is good practice to choose one method. It will create a professional look and uniformity across your blog.

This chapter was loaded with advanced topics related to creating an online store in your blog, however it is very advantageous. Giving your customers the ability to purchase your services or items for sale right from your blog will hopefully increase your sales by eliminating the need to leave your site to shop at eBay or Etsy, for example.

You can breathe now! The next chapter is on troubleshooting and where you can find additional help as your blogging skills grow.

■ ■ ■

CHAPTER 9

Troubleshooting and Blog Help

You've created your blog; published posts; added gadgets and images; altered the design, color scheme, and layout; integrated social networking tools; means of tracking visitor activity; added pages; and added an online store. Congrats! That is a lot to accomplish and I am so happy to have helped you build your blog.

However, in the future, you may have additional questions or may come across a few common mistakes. In this chapter, we'll review possible errors or problems you may encounter and their solutions, in addition to listing and providing an overview of supplementary help sites.

HTML and CSS Errors

Even with step-by-step instruction, you may receive error messages or run into problems. We all do! And that old saying is true: You learn from your mistakes. In this section, we'll review a few common mistakes and how to fix them.

First and foremost, if you are planning on making changes to your layout using HTML or CSS code, back up your current template by clicking the Download Full Template link in the Edit HTML section, which saves a copy of the template to your computer. If a problem occurs when you are editing the HTML, you can always revert back to the original by clicking Browse to upload the template previously saved and clicking the Upload button.

Case One: Right Column Disappears

You're working on your blog and realize that the right column (in a three-column layout) appears to disappear (when really it has dropped beneath all of your posts), and it was fine when you looked at your blog yesterday. What happened?

The most common reason is incorrect HTML code either added in one of your recent posts or in a newly added HTML/JavaScript gadget. If you recently added a new HTML gadget, remove the gadget and view your blog. If the blog appears "normal" and the third column is back in place, you know something is wrong with the way the last HTML/JavaScript gadget was added (maybe it is missing quotes around a URL address or missing brackets). Check the code you are copying for an external site and reinstall the gadget. If the problem persists when you view your blog, contact the author of the gadget, add a comment on their site, or check their Help section or user forums.

If you have not recently added a HTML/JavaScript gadget or by removing it has not solved the problem, the error most likely resides in a recent post. If you are copying and pasting code in your post content or HTML code from an external source, it may not paste properly or in error. In my experience, the most popular HTML errors in a post are a missing `</div>` or `</p>`. These are the closing tags for the `<div>` (division or section) and `<p>` (paragraph) HTML tags. Many HTML tags come in pairs with opening and closing tags, such as the `<div>...</div>` and `<p>...</p>`. These two tags are very similar in function and are used to format and style text in paragraph form. The Post Editor often automatically adds a pair of `<div>` or `<p>` codes when you press the Enter key while composing a post.

The problem is typically at the end of the post. While in the post editor, switch to Edit HTML view, scroll to the bottom, and see if there is an opening `<div>` or `<p>` without a matching `</div>` or `</p>`. If so, add it. Click Publish Post and View Blog to see if the column is back on the right side. Hopefully your problem is now resolved!

Worse case scenario, set the latest post back to Draft and view your blog. Continue until you find the post causing the problem (meaning when you click View Blog and the 3rd column reappears).

Case Two: Missing ";" in CSS Code

You're working in Layout->Edit HTML code view. When you save your changes, whatever it was you were editing has not changed as you expected. This may be that you forgot to add the ";" at the end of one of the newly added or modified lines of code.

For example, you may have tried setting the sidebar color or background color to white (which is #FFFFFF in hexadecimal coding) and instead of entering #FFFFFF; you only entered #FFFFFF. Basically, every line of CSS code needs to end with a semicolon (;) unless it is a comment (enclosed within /* and */).

Case Three: Malformed CSS Code

You were just working in the Layout section under Edit HTML, and when you saved changes the results you expected are not showing. First, check for the missing semicolon as described previously. If that is not the problem, you may have forgotten another piece of code. For example, in Chapter 7 in an exercise under the Edit HTML, there is a line of code to be inserted into your blog's layout: `border-left: 5px solid #000000;`. If you forgot the border width element (1px), no border would appear. It is also very common for people to forget the pound sign (#). If you need help with HTML, visit `w3schools.com/html` or `w3schools.com/css` for help with CSS.

Posting Image Errors

At times, people have trouble inserting images into their posts. Either they are too large or too small, or are not where they want them to be. First, go to Settings and under the Basic tab, Global Settings, you should be using the Updated Editor. It has new features to improve the image insertion process.

Case One: Float Image

Blogger has the ability to "float" images to the left or right. If the image being inserted is too large, you may end up with text running alongside the image one or two letters at a time, which is undesirable and difficult for viewers to read. If you wish to float images to the right or left (see Figure 9-1), be sure they have a width of 300px or smaller (or use the Medium or Small setting).

Waterfall in Upstate NY

A recent waterfall project
constructed in Upstate NY.
This beautiful lawnscape was
constructed by Mario's
Landscaping and supplied to me
for the purpose of The Perfect
Landscape blog and the
Beginning Google Blogger book.
Enjoy!

Figure 9-1. *Page layout*

Case Two: Image Size

Like most, you probably take pictures to be inserted into your blog using a digital camera. Your camera probably has settings for image taking where the default setting for most cameras is "large." These have a resolution over 1200px (which is far too large to be inserted into a blog post where the main posting area, on average, is between 400-500px). If you try inserting the photo into your blog without manually resizing it or using the Small, Medium, or Large setting in Blogger after the image has been inserted, it will not show completely in the post.

With the posting area between 400-500px wide, your pictures should be resized at no more than 400px wide as a general rule of thumb. If you like floating images to the left or right, I would recommend resizing your images to half the posting area space. If your main posting area is 400-500px, then for images you want to float, resize them to approximately 200-250px. You may resize images using Photoshop, Photoshop Elements, photo editing software that came with your camera, or online free photo resizing programs like ones found at `faststone.org/FSResizerDetail.htm` or `gimp.org`.

Image Issues

Separate (and in addition) to problems with posting images, you may have problems adding images to your sidebar (using the Picture or HTML/JavaScript gadget), banner, background, or other page elements. They may appear too large, too small, or simply just don't fit the way you'd like. To review the process of installing custom graphics, see Chapter 7. Table 9-1 lists standard elements and image sizes to use as a guide:

Table 9-1. Standard image sizes for Blogger page elements

Page Element	Element Size (W)	Image Size (W)	Notes
Banner (two-column format)	700px	680px	The image size is slightly less than the banner size to leave extra space/padding around the image. If you want the image lined up against the background without any space, the image size should also be 700px.
Banner (three-column format)	920px	900px	See notes above. Same logic applies.
Sidebar images	200-220px	160-180px	Make the images smaller than the width of the sidebar so it does not overlap any borders and to provide a better fit.
Footer	700px	680px	See notes above for the banner elements.
Post separators	400-450px	400px or less	This is an image that can be used to separate posts and must be smaller than the width of your posting area (described in Chapter 7, Figure 7-8).
Static background	N/A	1920px × 1200px	That is the size we used for The Perfect Landscape example where the banner is 900px wide. This custom background, although 1920px wide, has a white center of 920px wide, leaving 500px on each side (see Chapter 7, Figure 7-7).

Layout Design Tips

As mentioned in Chapter 4 when you began adding gadgets to your blog, more is not necessarily better. Your blog can become cluttered and disorganized very quickly by adding too many gadgets, where the user may get distracted from your blog's content. Here are a few layout tips:

- Choose only those gadgets that complement and add useful functionality to your site.

- Keep important information or gadgets to the top of your sidebars, such as the FeedBurner gadget allowing users to subscribe to your blog, as well as contact information.

- Limit the use of animated gadgets in the sidebar. Too many objects moving at once can be distracting.

Free Blog-Related Help Sites

Although we've reviewed a few common problems, I'm sure as you continue blogging you may have more questions or want to know where to find additional gadgets (also known as widgets) for your blog. The following is a list of sites I would highly recommend you visit, as well as a brief description of each site.

Blogger Stop (`bloggerstop.net`): A great source for articles and tips on Blogger relating to fonts and design, marketing, writing, and a list of recommended Blogger widgets.

Blogging Basics 101 (`bloggingbasics101.com`): Features tips on content writing, HTML help, microblogging, tutorials, and more blog tips and help.

Blogging Tips (`bloggingtips.com`): Helpful tips about keeping your blogging goals, search engine optimization (SEO) tips, using social media, and installing plug-ins.

Blogger Tips and Tricks (`bloggertipsandtricks.com`): Full of helpful blogging tips in general, including search engine optimization, CSS customization, HTML help, favicons (the small picture appearing in the address bar), hacks, and more, as well as those items pertaining to Blogger including three- and four-column templates.

Bloggussion (`blogussion.com`): Focuses on tips to become a better blogger including writing tips, blog design, SEO, blog marketing, and blog tools.

Daily Blog Tips (`dailyblogtips.com`): Enjoy a new blog tip every day! This site offers a daily blog tip from ways to drive traffic to your blog and making money to tips on creating a good post.

SEOMozBlog (`seomoz.org/blog`): All about search engine optimization and how to get your blog noticed best.

The Blog Herald (`blogherald.com`): An online "newspaper" about blogging using many types of platforms (including Blogger), social networking, wireless applications, and more.

Three Column Blogger (`threecolumnblogger.com`): Contains instructions on how to convert your Blogger templates to a three-column format.

Tips for New Bloggers (`tips-for-new-bloggers.blogspot.com`): Includes tutorials on how to add different types of sidebar items including a search box, music lists, and chat boxes, as well as blog templates, HTML to customize the look of your blog, and a section on publicity to help increase blog traffic.

Professional Blog Assistance

You can find a lot of help on the Internet and especially on the previously listed sites. However, you may not have the time to search for or experiment with installing new gadgets or modifying HTML code on your own and prefer to hire someone to help. The following is a list of services for hire:

Blogs by Heather (`blogsbyheather.com`): This is my personal blog and it contains many helpful articles on blogging in general, new tools and tips, and specific categories with one of them being "How To: Blogger." In addition to the free tutorials, I provide paid services including setting up your blog, maintaining your blog, converting it to a three-column format, transferring blogs, setting up a blog store, customizing newsletters, and more. I would welcome the opportunity to help one of my readers!

Blogger Buster (`bloggerbuster.com`): This site contains Blogger tutorials, templates, and up-to-date Blogger news. You may also hire Blogger Buster to customize and set up your Blogger site.

RemarkaBlogger (`remarkablogger.com`): Recent articles include marketing tips, how to deal with competition, and how to write better content for your blog. The main focus of this site is its blog coaching and consulting services. You may schedule personalized sessions and discuss topics such as increasing blog traffic, how to get more customers using your blog, working with video and audio content, and eBook planning.

Blog Design Services

Many people start out using a template when creating their blog; because they are learning and building their blog or because they cannot afford hiring a professional graphic designer. In Chapter 7, we reviewed how to install free Blogger Templates, where I am sure you may have found one to suit your blog. As you continue to grow your business and increase traffic to your blog, you may decide you want a fresh, new, customized look—a blog makeover. Here are two graphic designers I highly recommend:

Laycock Designs (`laycockdesigns.com`): Michelle Laycock is a professional graphic designer. She can create blog banners, backgrounds, animated GIFs (graphics), and advertisements. She can also create business cards, gift certificates, and other business forms you may desire (for print). Furthermore, she has designed coordinating themes for Twitter, Facebook, Ning, Weebly, Grou.ps, EventBrite, YouTube, and other social networking sites. Your blog and all your sites can share a common theme.

VK Design Company (`vkdesigncompany.com`): Veronica McCollum is another designer specializing in blog banners, backgrounds, buttons and badges, sidebar graphics, and more. She can also provide animated GIFs, social networking designs, and print designs (including business cards, T-shirts, banners, and key chains).

Both designers provide custom illustration and caricature design (a cute and fun cartoon image of yourself), and they offer a collection of premade designs for sale.

Summary

I hope you have found this book extremely helpful and I thank you for taking this journey with me. I know as you continue blogging, your blogging needs will grow and you may need additional help and have questions not covered in this Beginning Google Blogger book. In this chapter, we reviewed a few common errors, which are mostly HTML or CSS related, and we addressed image-related issues and a few design tips.

In addition, I provided a list of highly recommended free blog help sites which include articles on writing better blog content, learning new search engine optimization and marketing techniques, installing new gadgets, design templates, and more.

If you prefer to hire a professional to assist with your blogging needs, I have included a list of sites where you may pay for blog-related and professional design services.

In concluding this book, I am honored to have had this opportunity to teach you Google Blogger. In a nutshell, you have successfully created your blog, published posts, experimented with your blog's design, used CSS and HTML code, added numerous gadgets, reviewed search engine optimization tips, integrated your blog with popular social networking sites, and developed an online store! Congratulations! You did it! I wish you much luck and success in your future blog endeavors.

Index

▌ H

▌ I

■ T

You Need the Companion eBook

Your purchase of this book entitles you to buy the companion PDF-version eBook for only $10. Take the weightless companion with you anywhere.

We believe this Apress title will prove so indispensable that you'll want to carry it with you everywhere, which is why we are offering the companion eBook (in PDF format) for $10 to customers who purchase this book now. Convenient and fully searchable, the PDF version of any content-rich, page-heavy Apress book makes a valuable addition to your programming library. You can easily find and copy code—or perform examples by quickly toggling between instructions and the application. Even simultaneously tackling a donut, diet soda, and complex code becomes simplified with hands-free eBooks!

Once you purchase your book, getting the $10 companion eBook is simple:

❶ Visit **www.apress.com/promo/tendollars/**.

❷ Complete a basic registration form to receive a randomly generated question about this title.

❸ Answer the question correctly in 60 seconds, and you will receive a promotional code to redeem for the $10.00 eBook.

THE EXPERT'S VOICE™

233 Spring Street, New York, NY 10013

Offer valid through 11/10.